# A HYPNOTIST'S SECRETS TO

# Creating Charisma

magnetic personality
personal magnatism

## Gia Brainerd, PhD

ISBN: 1-4392-2817-5
EAN13: 9781439228173

Visit www.booksurge.com to order additional copies.

# A Hypnotist's Secrets to Creating Charisma

## Table of Contents

# Foreword

Why is it some people magnetically draw your eye and hold it long in a spell?

What invisible net captures your attention and your heart?

How can you walk into a room and everyone is filled with glee and awe?

People are enraptured—they want to be close to you. Enthralled, they listen to your ideas, words, songs, and stories. They love YOU.

This is truly a jewel of a book because it makes YOU enchanting. In it, Gia gives you the secrets of how to really win friends and influence people. This nuts-and-bolts step-by-step plan teaches you to develop your animal magnetism and have CHARISMA.

So get ready to tap into your innate wisdom and master energy and your mind to become a MASTERMIND. Read what Gia has to say. She knows a lot. Then take what she has taught you and put her ideas to work for you with your mate, friends, kids, and customers. The world awaits your magnetic magnificence.

Within seconds you will know how to be more persuasive and truly CHARISMATIC!

Shelley Stockwell-Nicholas, PhD
President of the International Hypnosis Federation,
www.hypnosisfederation.com

# Acknowledgements

To my family – Karen, Lee, Tim, Ned, Evan, and Drew – for not only being supportive of, but also interested in my work. Their thoughtful comments helped me put my ideas together.

To Shelley Stockwell-Nicholas – for her positive, enthusiastic influence and guidance, and for writing the foreword for this book.

To Risa Gordon – for her editing expertise and advising me of passages that needed to be rewritten or clarified.

To entertainers Nijole Sparkis and Kyle Vincent – for letting me pick their charismatic, entertaining brains.

To my doctorial advisor Alexander Docker – who challenged me to another level of understanding.

To my heroes Richard Bandler, Tad James, Milton Erickson, Dave Elman, Serge King, and Cesar Millan, who have all helped, in their own ways, to direct me along my path.

And to all my other friends and colleagues who have shared their thoughts with me, confirmed my theories, and questioned my concepts, allowing me to develop them further, simplify them, or better explain them.

May this book help and bless everyone who picks it up.

# Chapter 1
# What Is Charisma?

"The speech was nothing, but the man's presence was everything. It was electrical, magnetic."
– *A New York politician's observation of Theodore Roosevelt*

A few years ago, I saw a photograph in a magazine of Barry Manilow and a group of other people. I didn't know who any of the other people in the photograph were, but they all struck me as being extremely charismatic. These people were not communicating either verbally or with body language. They were posing as anybody in a family portrait would pose. Nothing unusual about the way they were dressed or any other visual component. When I read the description of the photograph, I found that these people were all country music stars – names that I instantly recognized, but I didn't know any of the faces. Yet, there was an energy that came across, even through a still visual image.

When I asked charismatic entertainer Nijole Sparkis about her thoughts on charisma, she offered an insightful description from her vantage point: "Charisma is the state in which you absolutely do not doubt yourself and what your purpose in life, or in any given moment, is. It is a clarity and certainty of what your particular gift is to give, and the act of giving it effortlessly from a state of complete confidence."

Studies show that we all form lasting opinions of people in about the first five seconds of a meeting. What can you learn about someone in five seconds? Being so instantaneous, it must be sensed at an unconscious level, even if you can explain consciously that a charismatic person is attractive or speaks well or has appealing body language. If you think about it, someone could still have these qualities, but not be charismatic.

Some think charisma is inborn and cannot be developed or that it requires certain social or behavioral skills. To most people, charisma is the "X factor," something extra that some people have, which cannot be defined, but we know it when we see it.

Even people who deal with charisma on a daily basis (such as those in the entertainment business and prominent speakers) often have very little understanding of what charisma is and whether or not it can be developed. Many charismatic people themselves are unaware of what they are doing to achieve charisma. Others may have learned or devised various techniques they use, but these offer only a glimpse of what is happening.

The reason charisma is so enigmatic is that in looking for a definition for charisma or instruction in developing charisma, charismatic people have been studied by looking for something that can be seen or heard, such as verbal communication, body language, and rapport. Exceptions can always be found, however, as many charismatic people are either not eloquent speakers, not aware of their body language, or do not attempt to create rapport. Referring back to my opening paragraph, none of those elements of communication came across through that photograph, yet charisma did.

The real answers are on the inside, where inquiring and analyzing minds can't directly observe or experience. The outer manifestations of verbal communication, body language, and rapport are reflections of the inner qualities.

I propose the following definition:

Charisma is a naturally occurring state, which can also be consciously developed, in which energy is outwardly expressed so that a person's inner power or radiance is strongly felt by others. Psychologically, the basis of charisma is having a self-empowering belief system, present moment awareness, a sense of purpose, management of mental and emotional states, confidence, a healthy self-esteem, decisiveness, and self-motivation.

Although that sounds like an awful lot of work from the standpoint of developing charisma, every degree of improvement in any of these components serves to enhance all of the other components, as you will learn and experience. Additionally, charisma is not all or nothing, as it may first appear. There are various levels, like playing the piano. "Twinkle, Twinkle, Little Star" is better than nothing. However, with increased knowledge, practice, experience, and persistence, you will reach the level to play Rachmaninoff.

Chapters throughout this book will detail the elements above and how they work together from different perspectives, offering various methods for attaining these magnetic attributes. Anyone can be charismatic with the energy expressed from the above qualities, no matter the line of work, whether passive or active, productive or destructive.

# Chapter 2
# How You See Yourself

> "What is necessary to change a person is to change his awareness of himself."
> – *Abraham Maslow*

To become charismatic, you have to first see yourself as being charismatic. I'm not saying that you will become charismatic *merely* by seeing yourself that way; however, seeing yourself with the qualities associated with your goal is a necessary step along the path to success. Put another way, you can't become what you can't even imagine. Imagination must be followed by action in any accomplishment, but imagination must come first.

Ben Sweetland (*I Can*, 1953) tells a story of a man he met on a train. The man had been a letter carrier for many years, and on his route was a mail-order house which received large bundles of letters daily; most of the envelopes contained orders with money. When wondering to himself why he couldn't be in business for himself and have a letter carrier bring important letters to him, the answer dawned on him: he realized that up to that moment, he had never seen himself as a businessman. He began to study a bit each evening and later embarked on a business of his own. When Sweetland met him, his business had grown to the point where he was taking a trip to New York to purchase merchandise.

This man had been a letter carrier because he had thought of himself as a letter carrier. As soon as he changed the mental image of himself, that new image began to manifest itself in his affairs. Sweetland later summarized, "The habits you have, which you would have liked to overcome, are with you, because you have not been able to see yourself without them."

Sidney Poitier, in an interview with Larry King, talked about how he became an actor. He had come to New York City from the Bahamas and made a living as a dishwasher, having left school to help support his family when he was twelve years old. At fifteen years old, he was between jobs and looking at the want ads for a new dishwashing job, being able to read only well enough to scan that part of the paper. Not finding anything available in this area, he saw an ad saying "Actors Wanted" and thought he'd give it a try. He saw it only as an opportunity for a job. In the audition, it became obvious that he couldn't read well enough to read lines from a script, and the director told him he was not an actor and that he should go find a job as a dishwasher! This brought Mr. Poitier the same realization as our postal worker in the previous story, and he made a decision, on the spot, to prove that he could become an accomplished actor. Of course, he did.

Granted, there are people who see themselves as charismatic, who are not. Likewise, the postal worker described above could have seen himself as a businessman without actually becoming one, and Sidney Poitier could have seen himself as a successful actor without achieving his goal. That's why this is not the end of this book. However, you cannot become charismatic without first holding that image of yourself.

People tend to focus on what they identify with. Therefore, when you focus on the charismatic qualities you want to develop, you will begin to identify more with these qualities and see places where you have already displayed these characteristics, and you will see where and how you can apply them to a greater extent in the present and in the future. People who focus only on their faults or how they don't want to behave will believe that is who they are and will notice every time they exhibit those faults or behaviors. They will fail to notice whenever they do something productive and the many opportunities that are constantly presenting themselves that will help develop their skills and charismatic qualities.

# Chapter 3
# The Significance of the Conscious and Unconscious Minds

> "My patients are my patients because they are out of rapport with their unconscious minds."
> – *Milton Erickson*

It's important to be clear about the distinctions between the conscious mind and the unconscious (or, interchangeably, subconscious) mind. In a lecture at The American Board of Hypnotherapy Convention (2002), entitled "Induction and Intent," Daniel Cleary explained, "The conscious mind makes decisions – we look, listen, learn, analyze, realize and critique, make judgments, accept and reject with our conscious minds. The subconscious mind runs all our 'programs' (whatever we've accepted) and bodily functions." In *Deep Trance Phenomena* (1996), Tad James simplifies the distinction further by saying merely that, "Your unconscious mind is the part of you you are not conscious of right now." This includes the beliefs you operate from outside of your awareness.

People go to hypnotherapists, or other therapists, because they have a problem they cannot solve consciously. Weight management, smoking cessation, and stress are very common reasons people seek out a hypnotherapist. The problem is at the unconscious level (if it were at the conscious level, people could solve it logically), and people who seek help (as well as many who don't seek help) don't know how to communicate with their unconscious minds to achieve their desired results. A hypnotherapist can assist in bringing the unconscious blocks to consciousness and effectively communicate conscious desires in a language understood and accepted by the unconscious.

The physiology, thoughts and mind-set, energy, and self-talk/speech, which all reflect a person's state and I discuss in Chapter 5, occur on the unconscious level. You do not consciously move each of the muscles in first one leg, then the other, in order to walk. That would be extremely awkward if you even tried. However, as in all behaviors, you had to first learn how to walk consciously. Once you consciously figured it out and your unconscious mind "got it" through practice and repetition, only then could you walk effortlessly and comfortably, and not have to think about what to do with your body whenever you had to get from point A to point B.

Likewise, your thoughts and mind-set reflect a complex history of perceived past events, past thoughts, and formed habits, but they too had to be learned (typically outside of conscious awareness, and often when you were too young to choose differently). It may not be easy to imagine how you can consciously change your thought patterns and mind-set, because they are so unconscious and ingrained; however, it can be done with conscious awareness, patient effort, and persistence. It's the same process as when you have to clunk out each note on the piano when first learning the instrument; after sufficient practice, the music flows out without your even being aware of how it is being created.

It's easy to see how you first consciously learned language and speech until, through practice and repetition, you no longer had to think about saying what you needed or wanted to say on a regular basis. Occasionally, though, when you want to say something in a certain way, you do think about it and form your words carefully. Self-talk, being an internal verbalization of inner thoughts, can also be brought into conscious awareness and changed.

Energy is perhaps the least conscious in our society; however, many people, such as shamans around the world, tai chi and chi gong masters, psychics, and energy healers, have developed conscious awareness of and sensitivity to energy fields, as well as techniques to influence or change them.

Many of the following chapters will discuss increasing rapport between your conscious and unconscious minds in various ways to increase your charisma.

✡ ✡ ✡

# Chapter 4
# Charisma as a State

"A magnetic personality is *not* something we can see
– but something we *feel.*"
– *Ben Sweetland*

Previously written descriptions of charisma include phrases like "a personal magic," "a special magnetic charm," and "appeal." These are all descriptions of what charisma looks like from the outside and give no indication of how it can be acquired.

Most people who assume charisma can be developed characterize it as a social skill, and instruct how to interact with others to be charismatic. These schools of thought differ from each other and sometimes even contradict one another. The authors or speakers are often coaching skills of a trade (such as how to be an effective speaker who can command an audience's attention or how to be a sharp businessperson who can influence others with negotiating skills), rather than how to specifically develop charisma.

If charisma is a state, however, it is not dependent upon interaction; you can be happy or unhappy without interacting with others. You can – and do – produce states in your own mind. Even when events or people trigger your state, it is really *your* inner interpretation and representation of that event or person that produces the state. People who are charismatic tend to be powerfully calm, focused, confident, self-motivated, and centered. These attributes all correlate to states and elicit certain feelings.

It's not always necessary to interact with someone to observe them as being charismatic. In some cases, a person can be perceived as charismatic simply by walking into a room. This may or may not be associated with body language. I've been aware of charismatic people entering a crowded room when my back has been to the entrance and I didn't see them, yet there was "something in the air" that preceded them and announced their arrival. In that sense, charisma is sometimes more than a state. When states are very intense and powerful, they take on an energy of their own and can be felt by others.

As to the outer social skills taught by others for developing charisma, I will go so far as to say that they will not have the effect of exhibiting charisma unless there is an internal shift in how the person sees himself or herself. Charisma must begin within, as it is a state and an outward expression of a self-empowering belief system. It is a personal power.

One reason I believe that charisma is a state and not a condition (the theory that either you have it or you don't) is that states are not constant. They fluctuate. And, if someone is charismatic, he or she is typically not charismatic all the time, under all conditions, with all people, and to the same degree, although we have habitual states in given situations. There are subtle degrees of charisma (just as someone who is in a happy state can be a little happy, very happy, ecstatic, and any degree in between). There is also the interesting phenomenon of entertainers who are charismatic onstage or on the screen, but who are not charismatic when they are not performing.

You may be charismatic in a small group of people you know well and are comfortable with, but may be "out of your element" when addressing a large group of strangers. On the other hand, you may be more comfortable with people who don't know you personally (maybe you can "create" a different identity for yourself, since they don't know any better) and really shine in front of a group such as this, yet feel uncharismatic with people you feel "know what you're really like." Additionally, there may be people for whom nothing you do is right, and you get knots in your stomach when you see them. Mustering up charismatic confidence in front of them seems to be a daunting task. Conversely, you probably know individuals around whom you can do no wrong, and you feel charismatic in their presence.

The term "stage presence," a manner that is thought to be charismatic or magnetic, supports this state theory by suggesting a presence that occurs during a performance, but does not occur when one is not performing. When discussing stage presence with musician Guy Guercio, his initial thought was, "It's made up of different aspects of the inner self all manifesting at once, tied together by the performance."

When pressed for details, he continued, "...Consider the following. Our lead singer is a moody, easily distracted person that seldom stays focused without prompting. This same man can take a stage and become a singular focal point for the audience for the entire show. He runs, dances, chats, and clowns for each ninety-minute segment. Once offstage and out of the public eye he reverts back to the private self, only to toggle again when he hits the stage. I don't see these transformations as false characteristics but rather the lesser-used aspects of who he is in total.

"I'm another example. Offstage, I'm the chatterbox and clown – on stage, I'm quieter and more intense. I don't think the intensity is foreign to my personality, but it is an aspect that only those who know me well get to see, and even they, only seldom."

Since you produce states internally, if you know how you create a state, you can decide to have that state immediately, or at any given time. With practice, you can call it up in an instant. Just think of a specific time when you felt charismatic (or powerful or admired) – any time at all; it doesn't matter what the circumstance was. As you go back to that time in your mind, associate with it; imagine being in your body at that time, and see what you saw, hear what you heard, and feel the feeling of being totally charismatic. Now, how do you feel? If you really connected with the feeling you felt then, you're probably in a pretty powerful state right now.

# Chapter 5
# Charisma Is Holographic

"A tentative person will walk tentatively, almost questioning the ground at every step. A jaunty walker often turns out to be happy-go-lucky, and so on."
– *Julius Fast*

There are four aspects of charisma: the body (physiology), mind (thoughts and mind-set), spirit (energy), and language (self-talk, as well as speech). These are all interrelated and each reflects and affects the others.

First, there is a physiology to charisma. If you imagine someone who is charismatic, you will know this is true. The way you carry yourself, breathe, move, gesture, and use your eyes and facial expressions are all ways in which you project how you feel about and see yourself. Others pick up on your body language either consciously or unconsciously and interpret your level of charisma and personal power.

Next, there is a mind-set to charisma. To be charismatic, you need an empowering belief system, confidence, and you need to know how to focus your attention and what to focus on. These will be reflected in your physiology and behavior.

Thirdly, there is a spirit of charisma. Aside from body language, we can sense someone with charisma, often without even looking at them. You have an invisible energy that can be measured with scientific instruments, which you connect with, feel, and express or project. Most people don't realize that they can consciously manipulate this energy and how it is perceived by others. Energy can also be affected through physiology and thoughts.

Finally, charismatic people use a certain language or language pattern. You know someone who is charismatic by the way they speak, their deliberate and unconscious choice of words, and the tone and rhythm of their voices. There is also a certain self-talk (the internal language and tone), that can't be heard by others, but which is even more important. If you are not aware of it, notice that you are always talking to yourself. Observe the conversation from time to time, including the tone of your inner voice. You almost always gain some insight you hadn't considered before.

Physiology, mind-set, energy, language, and self-talk will have their own chapters to discuss how to adapt and utilize them to express charisma.

# Chapter 6
# The Physiology of Charisma

> "The fastest way to change your identity is to change the way you move – your face, your body, your voice. Because [that sends] a signal to your brain that you're behaving differently, and it starts to get you to think differently."
> – *Tony Robbins*

We've discussed that charisma, as all states, encompasses the body, mind, spirit, and language, all of which are usually unconscious and on autopilot, unless we take them off autopilot and consciously change them. Changing any of these elements will change the others and change your state. To pump yourself up intellectually, however, is trying to make a change at the conscious level only; if you succeed, the results will probably be temporary.

Because your unconscious mind is in charge of the elements above, if you change one of those elements, and persistently enforce that change periodically, the unconscious mind will accept the new behavior and it will become a habit. An exception to this is when there is a belief or value held in the unconscious mind that opposes this change. That's why beliefs and values are covered in subsequent chapters.

You can look at others and know if they're depressed, excited, or angry – but how do you know the difference? For one thing, physiology. What is their posture? Where do their shoulders go? Where do their heads tend to go? Where are their eyes looking? How are they breathing – full or shallow? What are their facial expressions? When you start to become aware of your own posture, breathing, and other physiological patterns at different times throughout the day, you can start to make correlations with how you feel. Focus on different experiences and emotions you have had and notice how they affect your physiology when you relive them in your mind.

You embody your emotions. By first developing an awareness of your body, you can begin to notice the subtle emotional qualities you may embody at various times.

The body is more fluid than you might imagine. Norman Cousins gives a dramatic example in *Anatomy of an Illness* (1979) of a visit he had with Pablo Casals, an octogenarian at the time. Although Casals was best known as a cellist and conductor, he was playing the piano, flute, and violin by the age of four. When Cousins visited him, Casals had various infirmities that made it hard for him to walk, dress himself, and breathe. His body was stooped over; his hands were swollen and clenched. However, prior to breakfast each morning he had a ritual of playing the piano. This ritual changed his state in such a way as to actually change his physical form and ability. As he played, his fingers slowly unlocked, his back straightened, he seemed to breathe more freely. After a while, his fingers became agile and powerful, racing across the keyboard with dazzling speed, and his body was no longer stiff and shrunken, but supple and graceful and completely free of its arthritic coils. Your state affects our body, and your body influences your state.

Zen teacher Shunru Suzuki Roshi explains the importance of meditating in a posture in such a way that your body affirms, radiates, and broadcasts an attitude of presence: "The state of mind that exists when you sit in the right posture is itself enlightenment. . . [Sitting meditation is] not the means of attaining the right state of mind. To take this posture is itself the right state of mind." There is indeed a mind-body connection.

There is a powerful exercise that Tony Robbins calls the "cape walk." To do this, you walk around the room pretending to be wearing the long flowing cape of a king or queen, the cloak of royalty. If you were wearing this garment, how would you stand and move? How would you breathe? How does this affect your state?

A comparable exercise is taught in many NLP (Neuro-Linguistic Programming) classes, often referred to as the Superman exercise. Imitate the physiology of the Superman comic book hero, standing straight and tall, chin up, chest out, fists on your hips, and an imaginary cape blowing in the wind behind you. Imagine those bullets of negativity coming at you and bouncing harmlessly off your chest. Laugh a hearty laugh. Now, drop your arms, but keep that same inner feeling of invincibility.

Another exercise is to stand tall, shoulders back, breathe fully, look up toward the ceiling, and put a big grin on your face. Then, without changing any aspect of your body or face, get depressed. You have to keep smiling, standing tall, and looking at the ceiling. Your physiology is sending a message to your brain, and you cannot hold a conflicting feeling. A similar exercise that metaphysician and Huna instructor Serge King does in his classes is to go through a progressive relaxation routine, so that you are completely and totally relaxed. Next, he tells the class to get really angry without tensing any muscles. If you are maintaining a totally relaxed state, it can't be done.

Experiment with different postures, gestures, and facial expressions. Walk around the room the way you normally walk, to help you notice the differences in how each feels. Next, strut around as if you were successful, powerful, unstoppable, making the gestures and facial expressions you would make in this state. Now try the opposite. Notice how you would walk, gesture, breathe, and how your face would look if you were not confident, if you were unsure of yourself and what you were doing. Be confident again. Then try being bored and tired, and then sit the way you would sit if you had more energy than you've ever experienced before. Practice different states. Notice how each feels physically and what you have to do physically in order to achieve each state.

Then practice changing from one state to another by making physical changes only.

Charisma must be accepted by your body, which is ruled by your unconscious. By noticing what charisma feels like in your body, what your body is doing, what your mind is doing, and what your feelings are doing when you feel charismatic, you can practice accessing it at will.

✧ ✧ ✧

# Chapter 7
# Inner vs. Outer Control

> "A happy person is not a person in a certain set of
> circumstances, but rather a person with a certain set
> of attitudes."
> – *Hugh Downs*

This quote applies equally to a charismatic person. People who are charismatic or have a powerful presence appear to always be in control of any given situation. Of course, you are not in control of (though you may influence) actual situations, circumstances, or other people, but you *can* be in control of how you perceive where you find yourself, how you act or react in response, and how you utilize the situation. Effectiveness in this arena gives the illusion of being in control of everything, even when logic dictates that this is not possible. It removes us from a victim mentality and places us in a position of power.

Another point is that charismatic people do not typically attempt to "control," *per se*, but utilize whatever comes their way. People who attempt to control situations and other people usually do so because they do not feel any personal power or inner control. People who are charismatic, for the most part, realize that the only control they have is internal, and they work from that perspective.

There are two types of people with respect to control: those with an internal locus, or location, of control and those with an external locus of control, who place all control outside of themselves. Those with an internal locus of control know there is always something they can do to change circumstances. They can acquire knowledge or develop skills, they can take action, they can communicate with others, and, if all else fails, they can at least change their own attitudes and find ways to make a "positive" out of what was originally perceived as "negative" (this is called "reframing" and is discussed in a subsequent chapter). By the way, this last process is not denial. It does not say that there isn't a challenge; it merely finds a way of framing the challenge in an empowering, rather than disempowering, way.

Those with an external locus of control feel the situation is hopeless and that it's just the way things are; there's nothing they can do to make things better. They are the victims. They place control completely in the hands of others, circumstances, or even Fate. Sometimes "doing nothing" *is* the best decision, but only after other options have been determined and analyzed, *not* because you feel there is no alternative. Obviously, someone who feels helpless cannot attain personal power or charisma. You need to always believe that there is something you can do to make a difference. Without this important belief, there would be no reason to have a sense of purpose, and charisma would be out of reach.

Having an empowering belief system leads to a feeling of control. Although someone or something else may have contributed to a "bad" situation, it becomes your problem. As soon as you realize that, you get to figure out how to change the situation, rather than wasting time in the self-defeating mode of blaming someone or something else. Blaming others is a position of weakness, whereas taking responsibility is a position of strength . . . the position of all charismatic people.

In *Take Charge of Your Life Today* (2001), Lauren Luria equates blaming with using statements beginning with "if only." She gives the following examples:

"If only the bus had been on time, I would not have been late again to work."

"If only the chocolates weren't around, I would not be gaining so much weight."

"If only I could concentrate on my studies, I would be a better student."

"If only my mother hadn't been so critical, I would feel better about myself and be more successful."

She further explains, "Like blame, when we live according to 'if only,' we are letting someone or something else drive the car. Is the bus responsible for getting us to work on time? Are the chocolates at fault? What are we willing to do to be better students? And is Mother still responsible for our success or lack of it?"

The reason many people go to hypnotherapists is because they feel as though they are *not* in control. For example, they cannot control their weight, stress, or habits, such as smoking. Although a high percentage of people who consider hypnotherapy are under the false impression that the hypnotherapist will change them, if they are to achieve their desired end result, they must realize that *they* are the only ones who can generate this change. A vital role of the hypnotherapist is to show clients ways in which they are already in control and instruct them in new ways to utilize or experience control. Since they *already* have this control, and often are unwittingly using it to their disadvantage to perpetuate the undesired situation, they need to understand how their beliefs are serving or not serving them.

Society tends to take our power away from us right from the start. First, we are "controlled" by our parents or those who raise us, then by teachers and the education system, then by employers, the legal structure, and the government. We are taught about the power outside ourselves. Seldom do people learn about the power they have inside themselves. This is probably why the "civilized" world has so much crime, addiction, and abuse – people are rebelling against *being* controlled and looking for a way in which *they* can exert or exhibit some control in their own lives, even if it's destructive, causing harm to themselves and/or others. If they only realized the power they actually possess and how to access it, they could focus all that energy in ways that would be beneficial to themselves and others.

# Chapter 8
# Responsibility

"There are two primary choices in life: to accept
conditions as they exist, or accept the responsibility
for changing them."
– *Denis Waitley*

Charismatic people always choose the latter. The following
is a true story to demonstrate how there is always something that
we can do, and that taking responsibility to choose how we react
to and utilize a situation alters our experience. I went to see two
bands one evening. The first band, Rat Bat Blue, was a band I had
seen many times, and I had gotten to be friends with the band
members. The other band was fairly well-known and had a strong
following, even though they hadn't had a hit record in a number
of years. The bands were delayed close to an hour because of
technical difficulties. When Rat Bat Blue took the stage, the
first thing front man Ace Baker did was to offer their apologies
to the audience, even though the band had nothing to do with
the problems. Next, the lead singer made light of the situation,
pointing to his guitarist and saying it was all his fault (everyone
laughed and no one believed him). Finally, they dropped the issue
and cheerfully proceeded to give everything they had, putting on
one of their best shows. A good time was had by all.

Next, the "name" band walked moodily onto the stage and
never acknowledged that the audience had been put out just as
much as the band had. Their attitude was one of indignation.
They didn't drop the issue, but continued to the end to justify
their "sound" by the problems with the sound system. No one had
a good time.

The results? Rat Bat Blue had been told that because of time restrictions, no encore would be allowed. The audience had another idea and created a big commotion until they were allowed to come back. Polite applause for the "name" band, the one that most of the people had come to see, stopped before they were off the stage.

In the identical set of circumstances, which were beyond the control of both of the bands, and included the same audience members, one band wound up winning fans that night, while the other band lost the respect of people who might otherwise have bought their recordings or gone to future shows. Rat Bat Blue took the internal locus of control stance. They understood that although they could not control the technical problems, they could still control how they reacted to and utilized the situation. They stayed in the moment, acknowledging and interacting with the audience. They had a sense of purpose and intent – to entertain the audience. Did they manage their states? Absolutely! They were passionate about what they were doing, their actions presupposed charisma, and they were confident, decisive, determined, and committed. They were not attached to the problems, but focused their attention on what they could do to improve the situation. The levity they expressed raised the energy in the room, and they quickly developed rapport with the audience. They were magnetic.

The other band followed the external locus of control pattern. They were victims. They believed that circumstances controlled them, and they blamed everyone and everything they could come up with, without a single thought that there might be something *they* could do to make the situation better. They were not in the moment and did not say or do anything to connect with the audience because they put all their energy into being resentful and feeling "wronged." This also distracted them from any purpose or intent they may have had, and they certainly did not manage their states or access any feelings of passion for their craft or performing. With their energy so dispersed, they did not express confidence, decisiveness, determination, commitment, focus, connection to their energy, or rapport with the audience. Their attitude actually *lowered* the energy in the room. They were not magnetic, and I believe the majority of the audience most likely lost all interest in the band and never went to see another show of theirs.

From this example, you can also see the difference between having an empowering belief system and having a belief system that disempowers you (which will be covered in greater detail later in this book). You always have power; but you have to first become aware that you have that power in order to claim it and use it.

In a similar situation, singer Kyle Vincent did a show at a popular Los Angeles nightspot. The moment he stepped on the stage, the microphone went dead. As soon as that was fixed, they lost the amplification of the lead guitar. Yes, it was frustrating, but he took the opportunity to bond with his audience. He didn't leave the stage or lose his temper with the house soundman. He was uncompromising about getting the problems fixed, but while the system was being worked on and out of his hands, he talked to the audience, told stories, and kept the mood as light as possible. He was at his charismatic best and kept the audience in the palm of his hand. The way he handled the situation gained him respect from the audience, industry professionals, and the club itself, which later apologized and invited him to return as a performer.

In the late 1980s, I went to a taping of a talk show in which one of the guests (and the most well-known) was the legendary Steve Allen. The taping was in an old building in downtown Los Angeles, not a studio, and the equipment on-site malfunctioned. Other than to announce that they were having problems, neither the host of the show nor the producers were anywhere to be found, leaving the audience to twiddle their thumbs. No one had approached Mr. Allen, and he could have lounged in comfort eating and drinking the fare available to him, but he chose to take responsibility (which no one connected with the show had taken) and got up on stage, entertaining the audience for over an hour until everything was operational. He sat down at the piano, told stories and sang songs. He even took requests. This is the mind-set of someone who is charismatic. Charismatic people don't wait to be asked; they're always thinking about what they can do in the moment.

# Chapter 9
# The Cause and Effect Equation

"The sum total of all of your choices, both conscious and unconscious, has led you to where you are today."
– *Tad James*

The cause and effect equation says that you choose to be either at the cause or at the effect of whatever is happening in your life. Although we don't have control over people and events, as discussed in the previous chapter, and we certainly don't consciously cause the bad things that happen to us, charismatic people understand that all of the conscious and unconscious decisions they have made in their lives brought them to where they currently are. This is not assessing any blame. This is merely another way of taking responsibility and, therefore, coming from power in our lives.

It's very important to distinguish between being at cause and blaming. A lot of time can be wasted, getting stuck in an endless cycle of guilt and beating yourself up, when you take or assign blame. That is disempowering. The purpose of being at cause is to empower yourself to change an unpleasant situation.

In subsequent chapters that discuss the power of focus, you will understand that when you blame you focus only on what you don't want, and thus create more of the same. Being at cause is to decide to change your focus to what you *do* want, and thus bring about change in the desired direction.

Those who come from a victim mentality, being at the effect of whatever happens to them, have no power; they give their power away. However, if you come from the assumption that, although you may not have literally created the situation, only you placed yourself in that situation by your previous decisions, then you free yourself to have the power to make new decisions and put yourself in a different situation. You can change your mind about where you want to be, and therefore be at cause. Someone who is on the effect side of the equation doesn't have that choice. Power comes only when you are on the cause side of the equation. Can you imagine a charismatic person who is a powerless victim? Not likely. If you want to be charismatic, know that you are in a position to make and change decisions at any time you decide to in order to effect change.

This is one of the intentions of a hypnotherapist. When clients come to us with a presenting problem, they come to us on the effect side of the equation. They don't know how to change on their own. They don't own their own power. The hypnotherapist will give clients the tools they need to see the power that they have in order to make the change. It may not be presented in this way, but the hypnotist does not make the change in the clients; the clients are the ones who make the change, with guidance from the hypnotist.

✵ ✵ ✵

# Chapter 10
# An Empowering Belief System

> "The more files we have in our mental filing cabinet,
> which tell us something about ourselves, the more
> we will attract and accept other thoughts and ideas
> which support and prove what is already stored in
> our files."
> — *Shad Helmstetter*

Beliefs, which are our convictions about what is true, are not based on reality. They are based on our *perception* of reality; in turn, they form the basis for our perceptions of the world. Our unconscious minds use any previous experience and knowledge that can be associated to a given situation, and make an interpretation. If we already have a belief that can be applied to the current situation, our minds will instantly recognize it as a match, and not look any further. Unless we are challenged out of automatic pilot (either by new information that does not support the belief or by a conscious decision to develop awareness), we do not rationalize, analyze, or question our belief systems, how they were attained, or if they are even still (if they ever were) valid.

As an example, when I was in college, there was this gentleman I liked very much. One day I started talking to him and he just walked right past me without even acknowledging me. I felt rejected and probably developed a particular belief (made an unconscious interpretation) about how he felt about me and maybe even a more general belief about myself (perhaps that I'm not likable, that no one ever listens to me, or that people I like don't pay attention to me). The next day I discovered that his grandfather, whom he was very close to, had passed away the day before, and at the time I approached him he had just found out. If that fact had never come to light, I might well be carrying around one or more faulty beliefs to this day, based on that one incident that I had originally misinterpreted. Without the understanding that my previous thinking was in error, I might have lacked confidence in a number of areas from then on and not even attempted to go in directions that I eventually moved in.

We begin to form our beliefs at a very early age. Most of our beliefs are based upon what influential people in our lives, beginning with our families, said or did at one time (and while it may have been only one time, it is the aberration that we remember). Typically, we unconsciously adopt the beliefs of those close to us, because we assume (when we are too young to analyze or too inexperienced ourselves) that they know. When we are old enough or have gained enough experience for ourselves, our beliefs in this area are already set, and in most cases, we don't question them anymore. In growing up, most of us are taught about the power outside of ourselves and not the power inside ourselves, and so our belief systems do not empower us.

Richard Brenckman, in an article entitled "Change Your Channel" from *Avatar Journal* (1998), identifies beliefs as filters, or "a tuning mechanism in consciousness." He gives the analogy that when you have your television set tuned to NBC, all you see are shows on NBC. "You're just not going to observe any shows on CBS. No matter how hard you try. . . If you don't change the channel, you'll still be watching NBC. CBS will not manifest in your universe." He ties this to beliefs by saying that "when you observe or interact with life through a particular belief filter, only certain information gets through to you – the information that's aligned with the belief you're looking through."

Your beliefs really are *your* beliefs, no one else's. Even though other people may provide the information that you use to create your beliefs, no one else can *make* you believe something. That's why you – and only you – can change a belief that is preventing you from becoming charismatic or achieving any desired goal.

Having a self-empowering belief system is necessary before any of the other characteristics of charisma can be fully and easily achieved. In fact, all the characteristics that I've listed as being associated with charisma are based on our belief systems. Do you believe that you have a purpose, and if so, that that purpose is important and worth pursuing? You will only have a strong sense of purpose when you accept that there is a valuable contribution that can be made uniquely by you. People who feel they are "on a mission" are often irresistible.

Do you believe that you make decisions easily and effectively? If not, you won't allow yourself to be decisive. Do you believe that awareness of the present moment is scary or that it's uninteresting or that it's exciting? This will determine whether or not you'll feel safe or willing to allow yourself to be in present moment awareness. What are your beliefs about being passionate? Are you afraid of being "wrong" or judged by others if you display passion or strong opinions? Only when your beliefs are empowering you so that you feel confident in your own abilities and way of thinking and do not allow others to dictate or alter how you think or act can you truly exude a powerful presence and charisma. You can, of course, consider the opinions of others objectively and make a conscious decision to change your thinking or actions, but it will be based on your new perspective, not because someone else says it's so.

Most people's belief systems won't allow them to accept that they can be whatever they want to be or that they can do whatever it is they want to do. We must first discover what our beliefs are in order to consciously decide if we want to keep them, modify them, or replace them. Subsequent chapters will assist in identifying beliefs, and will offer techniques for modifying and replacing beliefs you decide to change.

✵ ✵ ✵

# Chapter 11
# The Role Values Play

> "If values are not aligned with the changes you made…then typically the changes will regress."
> – *Tad James and Wyatt Woodsmall*

Values, qualities we move toward or away from, are the ideals that are most important to us and propel our objectives and actions.

Charismatic people do not necessarily share the same values. What they do share is a congruency among their personal values and between their values and beliefs. Before you can align your values and beliefs, however, you need to know what your primary values are, as well as the beliefs you want to align with them. Discovering values will be discussed in this chapter. Discovering beliefs will be covered in the next chapter. After that, we will discuss how they affect our personal power and how to resolve conflicts.

Examples of values that we move toward are honesty, integrity, freedom, happiness, wealth, health, family, love, success, growth, contribution, power, respect, romance, communication, self-expression, passion, satisfaction, security, comfort, enjoyment, challenge, adventure, accomplishment, making a difference, intimacy, and friendship. You can discover your own top values by asking yourself what is most important to you and writing it down. You may come up with some additional answers, not listed above.

Examples of values we move away from are physical pain, frustration, anger, disappointment, failure, rejection, depression, humiliation, embarrassment, and loneliness. Again, by asking yourself what you would do the most to avoid, you will come up with answers that you can also write down.

These values do not carry equal weight though. There is a hierarchy of values. Two people can have the same top three values, but be very different. One person, whose hierarchy is "family, health, and career," will be a much different person than someone whose hierarchy is "career, health, then family." When you ask yourself which of the "moving-toward" values is most important to you, list the top three in order. Likewise, list the top three values you would do the most to avoid.

Values, like beliefs, originally come from your experiences with family, teachers, friends, work situations, and society, and rarely by conscious choice. If you behaved in accordance with values that were in alignment with the values of these people or groups, you were praised, rewarded, or acknowledged. If you behaved against the values of these people or groups, you were rejected, ignored, or scolded. You can also adopt values based on people you admire, such as role models and heroes. Your values and the hierarchy of those values changes throughout your life.

Values are important, because in order for you to be charismatic, your values must be aligned with your beliefs and goals. If someone's values and/or beliefs are inconsistent or conflict with each other, that person cannot have the sense of purpose, confidence, healthy self-esteem, decisiveness, self-motivation, and focus to manage his or her states and display charisma. This internal conflict is also a reason for procrastination.

If your most important value to move toward is success and your most important value to move away from is rejection, there's likely conflict, and you're probably going to continually sabotage your efforts toward success in order to avoid rejection. This is an example of having two different value systems. One way to resolve this conflict is to redefine the terms. Change the meaning of what success is, what failure is, and what rejection is for you.

Many people who are very focused on success set impossibly high standards for themselves and will not consider themselves successful even when the rest of the world places them at the top of the ladder. On the other hand, most people's definitions of failure make it very easy to fail. We need to use our definitions to make success easy to achieve and failure difficult.

Our beliefs are how we evaluate how we embody our values. People can have the same values, but different rules about those values. We discover these rules by asking ourselves, "How do I know that I'm successful or not successful?" Some people have rules that they have to make a certain amount of money, look a certain way, and other status markers. However, there are also people who are much happier, who say, "Every day that I'm above ground is a great day! And, if it's a great day, then I'm successful!" This attitude doesn't necessarily diminish motivation, as long as you believe you must continue to grow to be happy, keep setting your sights on new goals, and enjoy the process. Such a mind-set can be very powerful and relieve feelings of frustration.

You can also avoid feelings of failure by defining failure as "not learning anything from an experience." If you find you haven't learned anything, ask yourself what you *could* learn from the experience. Since your unconscious will always provide you with an answer (see Chapter 23 on "Questions"), you'll never fail.

Rejection, as all the other values, is not an absolute either. It's an interpretation. We may feel rejected, but that may have nothing to do with the reality of the situation. As with creating beliefs that empower you, you can also decide your own values and the rules (or beliefs) surrounding those values. You can set yourself up for success and empowerment.

✲ ✲ ✲

# Chapter 12
# Identifying Beliefs

> "It's important to understand that any limit to your thinking exists only in the paradigms ingrained in you, not in your potential or your ability to create a big vision."
> – *Loral Langemeier*

In the previous chapter, you identified your top moving-toward and moving-away-from values. Before you can analyze your beliefs, then reconcile your beliefs and values, you need to take a little time and effort to uncover and identify your beliefs.

You can look at your beliefs about charisma and charismatic people in general by completing the sentence: "Charismatic people are…" as many times as you can come up with ideas. Write them all down, so you can evaluate each one. This may tell you areas in which you view charisma negatively or as being in conflict with one or more of your top values, unconsciously preventing you from allowing yourself to become charismatic. You may be surprised at some of the issues that arise.

You may have a belief, for example, that says something like, "Charismatic people are egotistical." If humility is high on your list of values, there will be an internal conflict and you will not become charismatic as long as both value (humility) and belief (charisma equals egotistical) exist. To resolve this conflict, you can revise either your belief about charisma or your definition of humility, or both.

You may have known or seen someone you considered charismatic and who you also felt was self-serving, which caused you, either consciously or unconsciously, to decide that charismatic people were egotistical. Consciously understanding now that this is not a necessary element of charisma – that you can be charismatic without being egotistical – is an initial step. Think of examples to support this, such as Gandhi, who was considered to be both charismatic and humble.

On the other hand, you might also want to look at how you define "humility." If you grew up under the influence of, let's say, a parent who specialized in guilt trips, you may have had the belief instilled in you that the mere act of standing up for your own rights or pursuing a cherished dream was self-centered and inconsiderate of others. As an adult now capable of deciding what beliefs to accept and reject, you can see that this belief was distorted (again, consider Gandhi or other role models you admire). You can now choose a healthier definition for the value of humility, such as "being humble, realizing that you may not know the answers you think you know, and respecting the rights and opinions of others as being as valid as your own, even if they differ from your view." Once you formulate a new definition that you consider accurate and reasonable, you can accept that you can be charismatic and still retain the value of true humility.

Next, you can look at your beliefs about *yourself* in relation to charisma and various elements of charisma. Ask yourself the following questions. Do you feel you ever are or have been or can be charismatic? How do you feel about the present moment and do you feel safe and/or willing to allow yourself to be there? Do you feel you have a purpose? If so, do you know what that purpose is and do you feel it's important and worth pursuing? Is there anything you feel passionate about? Are you concerned about what others would think if you displayed passion? What situations are you confident in and what situations are you not confident in? Do you believe your ideas and feelings are just as valuable as anyone else's, without believing that they are more important than anyone else's? Do you make decisions easily and effectively? How committed are you to your goals? When you decide to do something, do you have the determination to see it through without encouragement or nagging from others? How much control or power do you feel you have in your life and in what areas? Do you often feel helpless or out of control? Do you feel comfortable being mentally and emotionally powerful?

Again, write down everything that comes to mind. Remember that beliefs are generalized convictions or presuppositions you have about yourself and the world. Make a note of those beliefs that you feel are unhealthy, conflict with being charismatic or other goals you may have, or otherwise need to be changed in order to serve you better. Future chapters will give many other techniques you can work with to accomplish this.

If you are not easily connecting with your beliefs or feel that there might be something you are consciously unaware of that is holding you back, accessing a hypnotic state (discussed in Chapter 17) can bring unconscious issues to the surface. In this state, you can ask your unconscious mind to unveil to you hidden beliefs that are limiting you.

Once you have uncovered your beliefs surrounding charisma, charismatic people, and how you see yourself, there are three questions that are helpful to ask.

1. "Are your beliefs currently serving a useful purpose in your life?"
2. "Is a given belief justified?"
3. "Is your belief based on complete and accurate information?"

Remember, beliefs are not reality. They are only your picture of reality. And that picture can be changed.

Many people have a belief that says, "Charismatic people are special; I'm just an ordinary person, so I can't be charismatic." If you study the histories of charismatic individuals, you will find that the majority of these people were not always charismatic. For now, it is enough to just be open to the possibility that you could *potentially* be charismatic. You don't have to believe it or affirm it; just imagine that it might happen. Just because you've "always" been a certain way or certain things have "always" happened to you up until now, that does not mean it has to continue that way. It is not your destiny or who you are unless that's what you decide.

# Chapter 13
# Reframing Beliefs

> "Successes are boring, because they only confirm what you already know. Failures are much more interesting, because they indicate where you can learn something new."
> – *Richard Bandler*

This is a good example of a "reframe." When reframing a belief, you find a context in which something you find undesirable can be viewed as useful, and therefore, change its meaning for you. This is a good way to work with some of the beliefs on your list.

Here's another example. In *I Can* (1953), Ben Sweetland recounts giving a lecture. A man came up to him afterward to say what a wonderful talk he had given and how valuable the information was that he offered. However, he said that he couldn't see success for himself. After some prodding, it became clear that the reason was because this man had done a lot of things in his life that he was ashamed of and he felt he didn't deserve to be successful. There are many other people who had lived with more integrity and who were more deserving. Sweetland did a reframe with this man. He asked the man that if he were to become an outstanding success now, would he use that success to make amends for his past mistakes. The man didn't hesitate to say that he would. Sweetland then put the question to him, "Wouldn't the world be a better place in which to live, then, should you take advantage of that which you already possess and make a great success in life?" The man had to admit that it would.

Most of our lives we're told (sometimes by ourselves) how we can, should, or need to improve or change. Seldom are we assured that we're doing anything successfully already. Whether we realize it or not, we *are* already successful; we're just not always aware of what our intent is or where we have our focus. When we're focused on what we're doing wrong, we often don't see what we're doing right.

Remember that Thomas Edison documented approximately ten thousand experiments for creating an electric light bulb before he found a way that worked. When a critic commented that he had failed seven hundred times, Edison denied that he had failed even a single time. He retorted, "I have succeeded in proving that those seven hundred ways will not work. When I've eliminated the ways that will not work, I will find a way that *will* work." He made a careful notation of the details of each experiment, so that he could refine the experiments that followed. Edison knew that each "failure" brought him closer to eventual success, because it provided feedback and was a learning experience.

3M's Post-it® self-stick note pads were a dismal failure of an experiment to find a permanent glue, yet nearly every office in America keeps a supply on hand. Someone found an outstanding way to utilize something that didn't work for its original intended purpose. This is an outlook that is common in people who are charismatic.

In the article "The Power of One Word" (*ABD Survival Guide*, August 15, 2001), Geoff Michaelson talks about going to a hypnotherapist to help him dissolve a writer's block he had when working on his dissertation. This therapist used the power of metaphors to assist Michaelson reframe his situation.

Michaelson expressed his frustration to the therapist and how the head of his committee kept changing things to the point where he was convinced the work would go on forever. He was stuck, convinced there was nothing he could do. The hypnotherapist zoned in on the first part and said in a very curious way, "Isn't it nice that things can change?" Taking what appeared to be negative, that the committee head kept changing things, he turned it around to imply that other things could change to effect a positive outcome.

Michaelson associated to all the good changes that had occurred in his life and to the wonder of many changes within the world, such as the change of seasons. Within a few months he completed his work and graduated in the fall of that year.

Here is that recurrent theme of control. This man felt that this situation was out of his control. Indeed, there were aspects  that he had no control over, and this is what he focused on, causing him to become stuck. Once his focus shifted from what he couldn't control to the possibility that he himself could also *create* change, he became unstuck and was free to function productively again.

✳ ✳ ✳

# Chapter 14
# You Make a Difference

> "Understanding the energy consequences of our thoughts and beliefs, as well as our actions, may force us to become honest to a new degree."
> – *Caroline Myss*

This leads to another widespread misconception. We don't need to *become* powerful. We *are* powerful already. Every one of us. I remember an episode of the television series *Fantasy Island,* where a woman comes to Fantasy Island because she's in love with this man whom she's been friends with for many, many years. She feels that he thinks of her only as a friend and she wants to have a "second chance to make a first impression." Her fantasy granted, they meet for the first time at their current ages. However, he's very different than the person she knew, as several major choices he had made in his life were previously inspired by her presence. In this scenario she hadn't been there to color his decisions. She found out how much influence she actually had in his life. (Of course, it all worked out in the end. Her fantasy was reversed, she was able to tell him how she felt, and the obligatory happy ending ensued. )

From personal experience, I moved to another state between my junior and senior years of high school. In my new school, I met a boy who was mentally impaired. I was nice to him, but didn't do anything special for him or treat him any differently than I treated anyone else. Years later, after I had moved away from home, my mother and his mother met. When his mother found out who my mother was, she raved to her about how much I had meant to her son. Other people he knew had talked down to him or made fun of him, but because I treated him the same as I treated everyone else, he didn't feel that he was "different" around me. I was not consciously doing anything to make a difference in anyone's life, yet I *was* making a difference. All of us are also affecting people's lives and the world in ways of which we are not aware.

You make a difference, whether you realize it or not. Even walking down the street and smiling at or greeting someone you don't know. That person may be going through a rough time; he or she may be upset, depressed, or trying to make a tough decision. If you smile and say hi as you walk past, you could change the person's whole state. It could create what is called a "pattern interrupt" and distract the person from his or her previous negative pattern to where the person doesn't return to it. You have influence on every single person and situation in your life in ways you may never know. That's powerful. You can use that power consciously by asking yourself, "How can I be more powerful today?" You will always come up with answers.

In *Anatomy of the Spirit* (1996), Caroline Myss told of a woman she knew who had a near-death experience and now views every choice she makes as having an energy impact on the whole of life. When suspended between the physical and nonphysical worlds, she reviewed all the choices she had made in her life, witnessing the consequences of each action upon herself, other people, and the whole of life. She was also shown that the spirit world was always endeavoring to guide her. "Whether she was choosing a dress or occupation, no choice was so insignificant that it was ignored by the Divine. In purchasing a dress she was shown the immediate energy consequence of that 'sale,' down a long chain of people who had been involved in its creation and distribution." Now she asks for guidance prior to any and every decision she must make.

✳ ✳ ✳

# Chapter 15
# The Meaning of Meaning

> "If you've identified now limiting decisions that
> you've got in your life, get excited! Because that
> means that we're on our way to a breakthrough."
> – *Christopher Howard*

You can create your own beliefs simply by deciding what they are. People read fortune cookies and bubble gum wrappers, and make wishes on stars, haystacks, and birthday candles, putting more faith in these whimsies than in logic. You decide what everything in your life "means," usually at an unconscious level, based on your beliefs and your perceptions of past experiences and events. These interpretations – positive, negative, or neutral – are extremely powerful.

Huna instructor Serge King uses omens in the third level of his course. At the conclusion of one of the morning sessions, he sends his students off to lunch and tells them that during the lunch break they will be drawn to something that will be an omen. They are then to interpret this omen. When I took this course, I was walking along a pathway when returning from the lunch break and saw a barbed-wire fence that had a hole at the  bottom large enough for a small animal to get through. I decided this would be my omen and I interpreted this to mean that no matter what restrictions there are, there is always a way out, a way to freedom. This illustrates creating meaning in something that intrinsically doesn't have any meaning. We could, however, say that the only meaning *anything* has in our lives is the meaning that we give to it.

The song "Bazooka Joe" by Parthenon Huxley demonstrates how we decide our own beliefs using the illustration of bubble gum fortunes. The first line of the song says, "Bazooka Joe says angels guide my every move and I believe him." Later, he observes, "So to this my life has come: there's meaning in a piece of gum," with a line from the second verse summarizing the very powerful fact, "We find convenient truth in whatever we choose." We will always find ways to validate to ourselves our beliefs or what we want to believe.

In *Personal Power!* (1993), Tony Robbins talks about breakthroughs, the moments in which people change the meaning of, or reframe, what's happened in their lives. People who have had traumatic events in their lives and experience feelings of anger, hurt, and pain or have the associated meanings of being violated or feeling that their lives are out of control, can create new meanings. The experience can now mean that they're stronger than they've ever been before, and they can now help other people. It can mean that similar events will never happen to them again because they know how to handle such a situation differently. This is also taking the internal locus of control – although the event cannot be controlled, the interpretation and utilization of that event can. At any point, we can take responsibility to turn the event into a powerful positive.

A process used in hypnosis called "pacing and leading" utilizes the words "that means." This is done by first "pacing" (giving the unconscious mind a series of statements that it knows to be true). For example, "You came here from wherever you came, you have reasons for being here, there are things in your life you would like to change. . ." This "leads" into a statement such as, "and that means that you are now ready to change and able to easily achieve your goals." Does it really mean that? We don't know, but the unconscious mind readily accepts this possibility as reasonable, especially since it was prefaced with agreeable statements. Politicians use this technique all the time.

# Chapter 15: The Meaning of Meaning

In *Man's Search for Meaning* (1963), psychiatrist Viktor Frankl relates his experience of being in a Nazi concentration camp, where he studied why few people survived while everybody else around them died. He watched and talked to these people to discover what made them different. The difference he found was their association to their experience in the camp. For most people, being in the camp meant death. They gave up right away. They focused continuously on "Why has God done this to me? Why am I going through all this pain?" The people who survived developed a reason or meaning for their suffering. Instead, they said, "I am suffering so that I can come back and tell this story to my children and make sure this never ever happens again on earth."

In *The Three Boxes of Life* (1981), Richard Bolles remembers listening to a doctor recount research he and some of his colleagues had conducted in order to find out why some patients healed faster than others. The research, conducted at a New York City hospital, paired patients who had undergone the same surgeries. In each pair, one healed faster than the other. The researchers tried to match the speed of healing with age, health, beliefs, optimism, and faith, but no correlation was found between any of these and the rate of healing. Then one day, through a fluke, the researchers got the idea of trying to match it up with "sees or believes there is some meaning to everything that happens to him or her." The correlation was virtually perfect. The more the patient believed that there was no such thing as a meaningless experience, the faster the patient healed.

We form (or decide) our beliefs by interpreting what an event or series of events "means." For example, when I was little, my father was a strong disciplinarian, constantly instructing and correcting us, because he wanted his children to be well-educated and have opportunities he never had. However, at the time, I interpreted his criticism to mean that nothing I said or did was right. I can look at that former belief now and understand both why my father acted as he did and why I responded as I did.

63

We have an intellectual need for everything to make sense, so our minds find meaning any way they can, though they can use only what they've learned and experienced up to that point. Therefore, many of our beliefs, unless regularly examined, are probably either no longer true or need to be re-evaluated in light of what we have learned since the original experience. Sometimes we make arbitrary connections as to why something happened or why it didn't happen, and it turns out that there was actually no connection at all.

# Chapter 16
# The Connection between Hypnosis and Charisma

> "Every practitioner of hypnosis will certify that success depends on your feeling of certainty, of 'I can.'"
> – *Kurt Tepperwien*

Both the successful hypnotist and the charismatic person must have a sense of certainty in their own abilities. Uncertainty will produce defeat in both. A genuine feeling of self-empowerment, which comes from certainty or confidence in one's abilities and oneself, makes a person magnetic.

Words like "mesmerizing," "magnetic," and "animal magnetism" tie charisma and hypnosis together directly. These terms were first used in connection with what later became known as hypnosis and have since been used to describe those with charismatic qualities. Before we understood what hypnosis was, Frederick (Franz) Anton Mesmer (1734-1815) – for whom the term mesmerize was coined – presented the faculty of medicine of the University of Vienna with his thesis on "The Influence of the Stars and Planets as Curative Powers" in 1773, claiming that the moon, sun, and stars affected the human organism through an invisible fluid, which he termed "animal magnetism." This substance, he theorized, could be derived from a magnet or loadstone, and he believed that all cellular structures have an affinity for the magnet.

Mesmer experimented with curing a variety of ills using magnetized objects, and later, due to a large demand, built a huge "baquet" which he filled with magnetized water. Those wishing to be cured would bathe in this water. As science eventually denounced his methods, the significant degree of success Mesmer achieved was later attributed to belief, suggestion, imagination, and expectation. These are now all known elements of hypnosis, and in fact, the present theory is that those states created by Mesmer in his clients were actually manifestations of hypnosis, presently categorized as hypnotic stages.

Today, those who exhibit Mesmer's qualities of influence through belief, suggestion, imagination, and expectation are said to be mesmerizing or magnetic. They are often thought of as being charismatic. Mesmer didn't need to use words to achieve results or exude power. His reputation of success preceded him, and those people who expected results were healed. Likewise, those who are considered mesmerizing or charismatic in current times can be considered magnetic without using specific language. This also explains why many people become charismatic only once they achieve a certain status. They may not be able to articulate how they changed, but because they cultivated a certainty of knowledge and abilities within themselves or others recognized them as powerful, an aura of authority and charisma developed around them.

✲ ✲ ✲

# Chapter 17
# How Self-Hypnosis Can Help

> "We are already in trance – clients come to us because they're stuck in a trance that no longer serves their lives. So, our job is not to induce trance, but to shift it."
> – *Dan Cleary*

Hypnosis is a natural state that you already experience every day. You briefly pass through this state when falling asleep and waking up, when daydreaming, and when absorbed in a book or movie. Hypnosis can help you develop charisma by overriding your conscious filters and assisting you in making shifts in your beliefs and behaviors at the unconscious level, allowing you to become more of who you want to be. It is your conscious mind that analyzes, evaluates, and says you can't be, do, or have the best. When you tell yourself (or others tell you) this enough times, your unconscious mind believes it and it is then reflected in your self-talk. You can intellectually convince yourself that your goal is possible or is within your reach, but it is the unconscious mind that now needs to be brought on board in order to realize change. And, if you have conflicting beliefs and/or values, as previously discussed, hypnosis can be used to get to the root of the problem and install a solution.

What is hypnosis? Medical hypnotist Dave Elman (*Hypnotherapy*, 1964) explains, "Hypnosis is a state of mind in which the critical faculty of the human is bypassed and selective thinking established." Let's break that down into English. First, we've already established hypnosis as a state. Next, the "critical faculty" is the part of us that evaluates and passes judgment, a function of the conscious mind. Hypnosis works because it bypasses the analysis of the conscious mind (what is and isn't possible for us) and communicates directly with our unconscious minds. You can do this for yourself using self-hypnosis.

Elman provides a simple technique for accomplishing this. First, close your eyes and pretend you can't open them. Then, while you're pretending, try to open your eyes. If you are concentrating hard on the pretense, you'll find that it is impossible to open your eyes. Of course, you know very well that you can open your eyes any time you change your mind and stop pretending. This is just the initial step, since hypnosis is not obtained until selective thinking is established by going through specific processes or giving yourself suggestions.

You can take yourself to a deeper level of suggestibility by imagining that you are at the top of a staircase in which there are ten steps. Tell yourself that each step you take will take you ten times deeper. Then count down with each step you take down the staircase until you are at the bottom. You can then imagine yourself in a comfortable room, sitting in a comfortable chair, at the controls of the control room of your life or being, or walk out a door into an ideal setting of your choosing. This will take you into a solid trance, which you can use for further processes or giving your unconscious mind desirable suggestions, knowing that at any time you wish, you can easily bring yourself back to a full waking state (to be described at the end of this chapter).

It is at this point, in the hypnotic state, that you can address your unconscious mind and request the answers you're looking for, such as what beliefs or values conflict is holding you back or how you can overcome your inner conflict. Then, just listen. You may remember events from your past, words that someone once told you, or ideas you had never before consciously considered. Save the analyzing and rationalizing until after you have finished your query.

You might find it easier to access buried information in a more objective fashion, by creating a "dissociation" (imagining that your unconscious mind is a distinct entity separate from you), so that the information does not appear to come directly from you. There are many imagery techniques for this and you will usually pick an appropriate scenario intuitively. Examples might be imagining going on a spiritual journey in which you eventually meet up with a shaman, angel, wizard, some religious or mythical figure – whomever you feel drawn to – and this person or being will reveal to you the information you need to know. You may also find yourself in a garden or forest and some animal or object that represents an issue for you will present itself. You can trust that whatever pops into your mind is right for you at that particular time. Using this type of imagery and story creation will also take you further away from your critical faculty and deeper into the hypnotic state, awakening your intuition.

When you are ready to come out of the hypnotic state, you can tell yourself that you will count from 1 to 3 (or 1 to 5, if you're in a deeper state) and when you reach the number 3 (or 5), you will be wide awake and feeling refreshed. Counting slowly, you become more aware of your surroundings with each number. You then open your eyes on the final count, take a couple of deep breaths, and then consider what you just experienced. Again, you trust that the messages you received are valuable. Your unconscious mind most frequently uses symbolism to communicate with you, which may take a little bit of unraveling to interpret.

As you tend to focus on what you identify with, you can give your subconscious mind suggestions under self-hypnosis, focusing on and identifying with the strengths you wish to further develop, programming yourself to imagine being charismatic and focusing on your own previous exhibitions of charisma. Shad Helmstetter proclaims, "Your subconscious mind is working right now, day and night, to make sure that you become precisely the person you have *unconsciously* described yourself to be." Through self-hypnotic suggestions, you can change the way you unconsciously describe yourself.

# Chapter 18
# Focus Is the Key

> "We hear what we listen for."
> – *Kermit L. Long*

Look around the room and notice everything you can see that is brown. Make sure you don't miss anything. After a few moments, go to another room before continuing to read.

Now, in another room, identify out loud everything that's in the room you just left that is green, then everything in that room that's white, and everything that's blue. Go back to the room now and look around the room, noticing everything you can see in that room that's green, white, or blue. You'll probably see many items you didn't notice before. Our reality is based on whatever we focus on. That is what's most real to us. The conscious mind can attend to only a very small percentage of details at any given moment, and we are constantly deleting, distorting, and generalizing information to accommodate what our conscious minds can handle. The external details we see are dictated by our mental focus.

I remember a story one of my college professors told us that demonstrates this fact. His daughter was a huge Michael Jackson fan, and when he went out with her, everywhere they went, she pointed out magazines and other items relating to Michael Jackson. These items were there all along, but he never noticed they existed before.

In one of Serge King's classes, he gave a demonstration where he had a line of burly guys linking elbows and a not-so-burly guy trying to get past the line to the other side, with the line being told not to let him get through. He tried in vain. Then

King followed this with a demonstration using the same people and rules, but with one addition. He pulled out a dollar bill and told the person who was to try to get through the line to pretend that it was a $100 bill. He then placed the dollar bill on the other side of the line. No one in the line even saw him get past them, it happened so fast! You can have a goal, but if you're focused on the problems, you won't be able to get past them to reach the goal (or, if you do, you'll be putting forth much more effort than necessary). If you focus on the goal, however, or the rewards for reaching the goal, interferences will not present an obstacle to you.

In another one of King's exercises, he had a student sit in a chair and another person stand behind the student and push down with all of his weight on the sitting student's shoulders. The student was then to attempt to stand up. Most people, including this student, try to stand straight up, pushing back against the other person's hands, and are unable to stand up. King then had the other person remove their hands from the student's shoulders and asked the student to stand up normally and sit back down. King repeated this last request, asking the student this time to really pay attention to how he moves his body in order to stand up. The weight is then put back on the student's shoulders and this time, standing up the same way he would without the weight, the student is easily able to stand up. The secret is that in order to stand up you have to push forward, not straight up. The weight of the other person was never an obstacle to begin with, but it was perceived to be an obstacle, and so it was resisted. When you spend your energy in resistance, you're not focused on accomplishing your goal.

In the PBS special *Inspiration: Your Ultimate Calling* (2006), Wayne Dyer told a story about one of his daughters going through a rebellious teen stage. Everyone in the family was negatively affected by her behavior, so they staged an intervention-type family meeting, each telling her how her behavior had hurt them. Her behavior got worse. Dyer then read a story about a tribe that lived mostly in peace. When there was a rare troublemaker, however, they would gather all the tribespeople around this person and each would tell stories about the wonderful things this person has done and how she has inspired them. Then the person can remember who she really is, rather than focusing on how her behavior has negatively affected her family and friends. Well-meaning parents who may try to motivate through criticism, often achieve the opposite effect. Again, you achieve your goals by focusing on what you want, not on what you don't want.

Dick Clark (*Dick Clark's Program for Success*, 1980) used an analogy to show that if your mind is focused on your weaknesses, you'll base your actions on those, and if you tune in to your strengths, you are apt to use them in dealing with life. "If you're worried that you'll drive your car off the side of the road and can't take your eyes off the ditch, that's where you'll end up. But, if you rely on your ability to steer, you'll stay in your lane and get to your destination."

Tony Robbins (*The Power to Shape Your Destiny*, 2001) also uses a driving analogy to describe a similar philosophy, making the point that the past does not equal the future, unless you focus there. Robbins states, "It's hard to drive in the future using a rearview mirror to guide you. You'll crash. You'll go, 'see, it happened again!' No kidding! That's where all your focus is."

People who are charismatic generally bypass figuring out how to solve their problems (what they don't want), and instead focus on figuring out how to achieve their goals (what they do want). You might say that a goal could be solving a particular problem. However, there's a subtle difference in that the charismatic person will be focused on the desired outcome, not the undesired situation to be overcome. Additionally, charismatic people have a sense of purpose, or an intended outcome, which assists them in choosing what their focus will be. Rather than focusing on what you lack, focus on what you want to gain. Remember when you thought about all the brown in the room, you didn't see all the green, white, and blue, even though it was there in plain view, as clear as the brown.

In *Conquering Procrastination* (1995), Neil Fiore tells a story about a boat that capsized in Lake Michigan thirteen miles from shore. Many people died on the spot, overwhelmed by the thought of swimming thirteen miles, and others died trying to reach shore. One twelve-year-old girl was the only survivor. She was found the next morning in the sand moving her arms and saying to herself over and over again, "I can swim one more stroke." She did the only thing she could do in the moment – she focused on what she *could* do.

# Chapter 19
# The Truth about Affirmations

> "For all our insight, obstinate habits do not disappear until replaced by other habits...No amount of confession and no amount of explaining can make the crooked plant grow straight; it must be trained upon the trellis by the gardener's art."
> – *Carl Jung*

What does this observation of Jung's have to do with affirmations? There are people who swear by affirmations, and there are people who say that affirmations are a "Pollyanna," unrealistic, ineffective, and even detrimental process. I have a theory about affirmations though. My belief is that the power of affirmations is not so much that the affirmation itself will accomplish a change, but that if we use affirmations appropriately and consistently, they can effect a change in our habitual focus. They can train our crooked thoughts upon our mental trellis if used artfully.

But, how do we use affirmations to our advantage? If we affirm our personal power, and then focus on our weaknesses and the areas in which we lack power, our affirmations will be useless. It all goes back to focusing on what you want instead of what you don't want, because the unconscious mind cannot directly process negatives. If someone tells you not to think of a green elephant – think of anything you'd like, but *not* a green elephant, a green elephant is what will instantly pop into your head. You can't *not* think about something without first thinking of it. Once you realize you don't want to think about it, you can choose to think of something else, but you have to think about it first. Your focus gives you your direction. Using affirmations, you can look at yourself differently, and move from looking at your times of weakness, to remembering times when you showed your strengths. When you affirm something that is not yet in your reality, your unconscious mind will guide you in the proper direction in order to attain this goal.

You don't get rid of darkness by swinging at it with a bat. Only by turning on the light can you make the darkness go away. You can decide that you don't like the darkness, you can analyze and characterize the darkness, you can vow never to live in darkness, you can have a majority vote against darkness, you can stage a protest against darkness, and you can wage war on darkness. None of these decisions or actions will abolish the darkness, which is merely an absence of light. You must seek the positive reality, light, in order to be free from the darkness.

In *Inspiration: Your Ultimate Calling* (2006), Wayne Dyer explains, "When we approach a long food buffet, we don't focus on eliminating the things we don't want; instead, we begin to vibrate in our thoughts to what we *do* want and ignore what we don't."

In hypnotherapy, we refocus our clients' thoughts from their undesired habits to the habits they wish to express in their place. People who seek help through hypnosis are generally dissatisfied with something in their lives. The effective hypnotist finds out what the client *does* want and helps the client to focus on and attain *that* goal.

If you're thinking that focusing on the positive is just not being realistic, consider a metaphor given by Tony Robbins in *Personal Power!* (1993) about being at a party. If you were looking through a camera that was focused on one little portion of the party, would you think that little part was truly the party? Not only would that be inaccurate, but consider that the camera may even create close-ups, making things bigger or brighter or worse than they actually are. Your brain does the same thing. We delete, distort, and generalize to reduce the tremendous amount of information coming into our environment at any given time.

There's enough going on in the party of your life, Robbins summarizes, that you could always find something to be upset about if you focus on areas that don't match your expectations, and make them big and bright and close (this is an example of an internal representation). Most people are good at taking undesirable areas of their lives and blowing them out of proportion. However, it's equally true that at virtually any party, at any moment in time, there's somebody having a good time. You could just as easily focus on some area of your life that's great and make yourself feel wonderful. You could also take some little thing, something that's just nice, and make it bigger and brighter and immediately feel better about it as well. Changing your internal representation of an event, which we will discuss in the next chapter, can change how you feel about it.

There is tremendous power in controlling the focus of your mind. There are two results you can control in terms of focus. You can control *what* you're focusing on (what you're picturing in your mind, saying to yourself, paying attention to), and you can control *how* you're focusing (your internal representation of what you're focusing on, which will be discussed in greater detail in the next chapter, Chapter 20). The same is true of affirmations; you control what you are affirming, as well as how you are affirming it.

The most important times to use affirmations to your advantage are the times when you naturally pass through the hypnotic stage – as you're falling asleep at night (which has the added benefit of allowing your unconscious mind to focus on, and help you to move toward, the positive while your conscious mind sleeps), and as you're coming awake in the morning (which assists in getting your day started on the right foot).

As for *how* you focus on affirmations, you don't recite them mindlessly. Affirmations are to be *affirmed*, delivered with integrity of emotion. Really think about each word as you say it, and imagine feeling it from the inside out. There are three affirmations I recommend starting your day with and repeating whenever you feel you are off track and need to correct yourself: "I feel good; I feel *great*. It's a wonderful day."; "I have the power to reach my goals, and I reach them."; and "Today I do only those things that promote my goals." Those are my favorites, but as you practice, you'll find your own favorites. That is how you can use affirmations to help direct and maintain your focus.

# Chapter 20
# Your Internal Representation of Charisma

> "The person with low self-esteem discards the positive while actually 'enlarging' and 'enhancing' those tape sequences containing unfavorable personal information."
> – *Marilyn Sorensen*

This quote is an example of an undesirable focus and how a self-image can become distorted, unconsciously. In the previous chapters we discussed the importance of focus and *what* to focus on. Remember, I said that you could also decide *how* you focus. This chapter will discuss how you can add *charisma* to your internal representations.

Your mind has a way that it codes information in your life – every person, place, and thing, every experience and event, every feeling and state. Each outer modality of sight, sound, touch, taste, and smell has a corresponding inner modality that makes up how you represent everything internally, the language of your unconscious mind. There is an additional inner modality of self-talk, which is the internal narrative or dialogue constantly running to explain, interpret, and evaluate what you experience to yourself. Your unconscious mind receives suggestions through your self-talk. As you become more aware of your self-talk, what you're telling yourself about your experiences, you can better understand your feelings and behavior. Chapters 21 and 22 will go into language and self-talk in greater detail and assist you in changing these powerful suggestions.

Remember the camera-at-the-party analogy? That story and the quote at the beginning of this chapter also describe how events and feelings are internally represented using "submodalities" – the properties of our inner modalities of vision (size, distance, location, brightness, black and white/color, still picture/movie, association/ dissociation – whether you are in the picture or watching yourself in the experience), sounds (volume, location, distance, tempo, tone/timbre, pitch), and touch/feeling (location, as well as temperature, hard or soft, sharp or smooth, pain or pleasure, and degrees of pressure, and also emotions).

Doe Lang (*The New Secrets of Charisma*, 1999) notes, "When you make changes in the way you *imagine* your life and its meaning, your ability to affect others' lives grows powerfully and dramatically." The influence of charismatic people often stems from their inner vision, which they unconsciously project. This causes others to unconsciously respond in kind.

Begin thinking about experiences, emotions, and beliefs, and deciphering how your brain encodes these thoughts and feelings. When you see images associated with memories, emotions, and beliefs, go through and find the submodalities associated with the images. Then do the same for sounds and internal dialogue. Notice any kinesthetic (physical or emotional) sensation connected with these thoughts and feelings, and notice if any smells or tastes are involved. Play with the submodalities and see what happens when you turn up the brightness, change the location, or turn the volume up or down, for example. Notice how it changes the way you experience the memory, belief, or emotion.

Now, think about charisma. What images, sounds, and sensations arise for you? Do you see sparkling lights around you like stars, lightning bolts, fireworks, footlights, or spotlights? What is your image of how you, being charismatic, would look, breathe, and present yourself? Do you see yourself with twinkling eyes, a beaming face, a radiant personality – friendly, cheerful, laughing, and sparkling?

What about sounds? Do you hear a particular soundtrack – music that is mesmerizing, motivating, or regal? Do you hear applause and cheers or people talking to or about you in awe, with lots of compliments, and perhaps saying how you've affected their lives in wonderful ways?

Now for feelings. Do you feel confident, powerful, focused, purposeful, centered, or serene?

What about submodalities? Do you see yourself in the picture or are you experiencing it within, as being a part of the picture? Bring the picture closer, make it larger, make it brighter and more colorful, turn up the volume if it's too soft or far away (or bring the sound closer), make the sounds more passionate, make the feelings more intense. Play with all of the different elements until you feel more charismatic than you've ever felt before. Consider beginning and ending your days with this exercise.

✵ ✵ ✵

# Chapter 21
# How Language Affects Your State

> "What if, instead of considering this 'wasted' time,
> you shifted your response and considered the wait
> 'found' time – a surprise gift, like finding a ten-dollar
> bill in the pocket of a coat you haven't worn since
> last year?"
> – *Stephan Rechtschaffen*

This is an example of reframing by changing your language, which Rechtschaffen recommends when in a situation where you have to wait in line or wait for a phone call or meeting, or spend unplanned time commuting.

Tony Robbins tells a story in *The Power to Shape Your Destiny* (2001) that is quite thought provoking. He and two business associates were negotiating a deal with another company that was taking advantage of them. Robbins, when alone with his two associates, noticed how each of them had a drastically different reaction. He himself was angry and upset, but still in control; one of his associates was livid and out of control; and the other associate was very calm. Robbins tried calming down his first associate, and noticed the state of his other associate. He then realized what an interesting phenomenon this was. The three of them were in the identical position with the identical trigger, identical stimulus, yet totally different emotional reactions. He also became aware that each of them used different words. He used the words "angry" and "mad," the first associate used the words "in rage" and "furious," and the other associate used the words "annoyed" and "peeved." Could the words we use affect our state?

Robbins translated this experience to other situations he encountered. He watched himself and those close to him, changing his own words, and advising others to change their habitual words, to see what else would change. The results of this experiment were astounding. One example is a friend of his who was always easygoing and even-tempered. His wife was dumbfounded when he uncharacteristically lost his temper completely one day. He explained that he was "overwhelmed." His wife laughed and said that wasn't his word, it was their daughter's word. He had never used that word before, yet their daughter used it occasionally and was in an emotional state when she did. Robbins found this interesting, and had his friend cut that word from his vocabulary and come up with a couple of alternate words to use in its place – words that would be more useful. He did, and returned to his usual easygoing self.

This particular story affected me, as I had been using the words "overwhelmed," "swamped," and "buried" around that time, an extraordinarily hectic time at my workplace. I felt mentally and emotionally out of control. I decided to do my own experiment. Every time one of those words entered my mind, I replaced it with "I'm on top of it," "I can handle it," and "everything's under control." To my amazement, these sentiments quickly began to be reflected in my reality.

Notice the words you habitually use, both spoken and in internal dialogue, and notice what happens if you deliberately change your words to ones that relate to a more useful or empowering state. When beginning this process, you might want to write down words you tend to use that "reflect," or perhaps even cause, your emotional state.

Thich Nhat Hanh, in *The Present Moment* (1994), describes what he refers to as "telephone meditation": when the phone rings, it "calls" you back to the present moment. Since reading this, whenever the phone rings, I say to myself, "wake up call!" It helps me to re-evaluate my focus at the time.

# Chapter 21: How Language Affects Your State

Another way of changing your internal dialogue from an automatic response when something goes "wrong" is to immediately transform that thought into, "That's good." Then you can figure out why it's good, or how the situation can be utilized so that something positive or useful can come from it. If you immediately start out thinking the situation is bad, you won't consider how it might be perceived in a different way. Once you condition yourself to start with this new premise, it's easy to come up with a positive perspective, but not until you release your limited thinking and look for alternate viewpoints. Charismatic people typically think outside the box and are always on the lookout for opportunities to make their lives more positive and productive.

# Chapter 22
# Self-Talk – Everyone Does It

> "What we say to ourselves dictates how we feel, what we believe, and ultimately what we do…It is actually here in our minds that we form our interpretations and give ourselves feedback, through our inner voice."
> – *Marilyn Sorensen*

Whether or not we are aware of it, we talk to ourselves constantly, making comments about the things we observe in others and the things we see in ourselves. Most people are not aware of the profound effect of this personal monologue. We review and rate ourselves through self-talk, producing turmoil and anxiety, or quieting our fears and encouraging confidence.

Since you know that two people can have the same experience or observe the same event and come away with very different conclusions or emotions, you can understand that these conclusions or emotions are dependent upon their cognitive interpretations, often based on past experiences, which then become embedded in self-talk. In other words, emotions do not come as the result of an observation or an experience in itself, but rather as the result of the things we say to ourselves about those observations or experiences. First, you always have a focus, though you're not always aware of where that focus is. Listening to your self-talk is one way that can show you where your focus is. You might be telling yourself what you want, what you don't want, that you don't know what you want, or you might simply repeat the same thoughts day in and day out, without any direction at all.

Once you are aware of your self-talk, you can manage your focus by deciding what you want and directing your own attention. Believe it or not, you really can choose to think about what you want to think about! Most people just don't take that initiative very often. Some people, however, decide they *don't* want to think about a particular thing. Well, you know *that* doesn't work! They can't stop thinking about it!

You can decide *what* to focus on, *how* you focus on it (explained in the next chapter), and you can also *interpret* ("frame" or "reframe") what you are focusing on. Shad Helmstetter (*What to Say When You Talk to Your Self*, 1982) explains how you can successfully ruin an entire day by allowing even a single event to create the first step in a negative cycle. "This negative cycle is not caused by the problem or event that appears to set it off – the cycle begins with how you *respond* to the problem in the first place." To your subconscious mind, they are exactly as bad as you perceive them to be, and as bad as you tell yourself that they are. When something happens in your life that you did not anticipate, instead of thinking of it as a disaster, you can change not only your words, but also your interpretation, and focus on how this event could improve your life or how it might show you some strength or ability you didn't realize you had.

Another aspect of self-talk is the "critical voice" we all have in our heads from time to time (some more often than others). In *Personal Outcomes: Motivation* (1989), Richard Bandler consulted with a man driven to stutter because of a destructively critical voice in his head. In this instance, Bandler's wisdom told him not to get rid of the voice or change what the voice was saying. "You don't want to turn off critical voices, because often they're right. It's just because of the way they talk to you, you don't want to listen to them," Bandler explained. It turned out that he was right and that the voice really did have a positive intention. Altering submodalities, as we discussed in Chapter 20, he proceeded to have the young man change the voice's tone (from stern and shrill to sweet and sexy), soften the volume of the voice, and change the direction from which the voice seemed to project, all with positive results.

When that nagging voice comes through for you, try changing the tone to that of a sexy voice, or another non-threatening, even playful voice (I changed mine to Dudley Do-Right). This will change your state by interrupting your negative pattern, and it will allow you to actually listen to what that voice is saying – whether it's just an old "tape" or it's telling you something of value. We often habitually tune out our unconscious thoughts. Start listening to yourself more closely, and you might learn some things that will help you achieve your goals more easily. Charismatic people do.

✫ ✫ ✫

# Chapter 23
# What Questions Do You Ask Yourself?

> "The quality of your life comes down to the quality of the questions you ask yourself on a daily basis."
> – *Tony Robbins*

This "quality of your life" includes your level of charisma and personal power. Until you think about it, you may not realize that in everything you do throughout the day, you're asking yourself questions and making decisions based on those questions.

The questions you ask yourself (a form of self-talk) are another way to manage your focus and your state. You might ask yourself a question such as, "Why can't I ever get anything done?" There are three problems with this kind of question. First, as we've discussed, it focuses on the negative – you're thinking about what you *don't* want instead of what you *do* want. Secondly, hypnotherapists know that the unconscious mind will work to answer these questions, by using past input – what people have said to you in your life, what you've said to yourself, and what you've read or seen on TV. Therefore, it would be more productive and inspiring to ask, "How can I accomplish my goals quickly and easily and make a game out of it?" So, if you ask yourself, "Why am I so stupid?" or "Why do these things always happen to me?" your unconscious mind will come up with answers. However, if you focus on how to make better decisions or what you want to happen and how to make that happen, those will be the answers that will be forthcoming. Ask a lousy question, and you'll get a lousy answer. However, if you ask a better quality question, you will get a better quality answer.

The third problem with questions like, "Why can't I get anything done?" "Why am I so stupid?" or "Why do these things always happen to me?" is that they contain hidden presuppositions. Presuppositions, which will be covered in detail later in this book, are assumptions (which may or may not be true) upon which you base your subsequent thoughts and actions. For example, "Why can't I get anything done?" presupposes, or assumes, that you don't get anything done. This isn't universally true; there *are* some things that you *do* get done. But when you word it that way, your brain stops evaluating whether it's true or not, and instead just looks for an answer. Once you realize that, it becomes easier to see what it is that isn't getting done and decide how to do it.

Many of the questions you ask are habitual. They are on an automatic level and you don't even realize they are going on inside your head. For instance, if the first thing on your mind when you wake up is, "Do I have to get up *now*?" that's not a very good way to start your day or focus. Listen to your habitual questions and come up with some good, empowering alternatives you can use the next time they come up. Soon you'll be able to see that your questions also determine how you feel. If you have certain habitual feelings that you don't like, those feelings are coming from what you habitually focus on. And what you habitually focus on comes from the habitual questions you ask yourself.

You can come up with some new discoveries about yourself and the world you live in if you come up with some new questions. Some good examples of questions that charismatic people ask themselves are, "What could I learn from this?" "What goals would I set if I knew I couldn't fail?" and "What am I doing right?" These are power questions. A hypnotherapist might have you ask your unconscious mind (sometimes in the guise of a "part," discussed in Chapter 28, or a "wise being," like an angel or a shaman) ways in which you can achieve what you desire. It can be very powerful and insightful if you initiate the answers or visualize yourself in this state, rather than analytically from the conscious mind. If you have difficulty coming up with a solution, you can "project" yourself (in hypnosis or self-hypnosis) into the future and ask yourself how you attained the goal. This presupposes that the issue was solved.

For charisma, ask yourself the following questions and, without judgment, listen to the responses that come from inside: "In order to communicate charisma or personal power, what do I have to believe? What do I have to tell myself? What are the pictures in my mind? and how are the beliefs, sounds, pictures, and language represented internally?"

As another powerful way of using questions, instead of asking yourself the potentially overwhelming question of, "What should I do?" try asking, "What will I regret not having done at some future date?" In *Wherever You Go, There You Are* (1994), Jon Kabat-Zinn advises "listening to the thinking that your questioning evokes, as if you were sitting by the side of the stream of your own thoughts."

✡ ✡ ✡

# Chapter 24
# Awareness of Energy

> "Every atom is more than 99. 9999 percent empty space, and the subatomic particles moving at lightning speed through this space are actually bundles of vibrating energy. These vibrations aren't random and meaningless, however; they carry information."
> — *Deepak Chopra*

Until recently, discussion of energy was considered to be in the realm of the mystical. However, with the discovery of neurotransmitters and neuro-peptides in the 1970s and medical research by esteemed physicians such as Candice Pert and Deepak Chopra, the interrelatedness of thoughts, energy, and matter are being accepted as well-established. Humans are electromagnetic by nature. When you physically feel "electricity" or "magnetism," that's who you are. That means you have present moment awareness.

Chopra's *Quantum Healing* (1989), which explains that our bodies are comprised of energy and information, is a landmark work that details and supports many breakthroughs in the field of mind-body-environment relatedness and medicine. Scientific instruments used by brain researchers (in a procedure known as positron-emission tomography, or PET) can now show that whenever we change our thoughts and feelings, our body's chemistry literally changes simultaneously and neuro-peptides appear, disappear, and change their paths according to our thoughts. Some people with multiple personalities have been documented to have one personality with moles, allergies, or disorders, such as diabetes, while the other personalities do not. When the personality changes, the physiological change is instantaneous.

Our energy fields, which are more fluid than our bodies, but less fluid than our thoughts and feelings, appear to be the link between our thoughts and our bodies. If our thoughts change our physiology, and our bodies are comprised of energy, then changing our thoughts must also change the energy fields. Charisma doesn't require physical presence, as our energy can travel with our thoughts and be felt over a phone, radio, or recording.

States, being expressions of energy, can also be translated into feelings. When you are charismatic, you *feel* charismatic. Energy can be expressed along a spectrum of open to closed, with accompanying feelings. When you feel love, joy, happiness, creativity, or freedom, your energy has a feeling of being expanded or open (directed outward) and free flowing. When you feel fear, hate, anger, procrastination, or depression, your energy has a feeling of being contracted, constricted, or closed (directed inward) and blocked. When your energy is expanded, you feel charismatic and magnetic. You feel connected to and a part of everything and everyone, attracting people and events. When your energy is contracted, you feel disconnected and alienated, repelling or cutting yourself off from people and events. The fewer mental, emotional, and physical tensions you have, which also close off and block energy, the more powerful and charismatic your energy will be.

Energy is felt throughout and around the entire body and, when fully in the present moment, it is expressed through the eyes. The best actors can make you feel what their characters feel without saying a word. All you have to do is look at their eyes, the windows to the soul, which fully express the inner feelings their characters are conveying.

When energy is charismatic, it can be felt without touch, indicating that our energy fields, or energy bodies, extend beyond our physical bodies. The more charismatic a person is, the further their energy can be felt by others. This can be done with thought and by intention (Chapter 26). Charismatic speakers or entertainers will often encompass the entire room with their energy. You must first become aware of your energy, however, before you can expand it well beyond your physical being. There are several ways to develop awareness of your energy. Since your energy body is interconnected with your physical body – at least as long as you are in the physical realm – a good first step is to develop a higher awareness of your physical senses.

One way is to become aware of your breathing. Feel your breath enter your nose, travel to your lungs, come back up, and leave through your nose. Being very still will help you develop more sensitivity. You might even feel as if your entire body is breathing.

Another way is progressive relaxation, where you focus on one part of your body at a time, and progress from one end to the other. It's an individual preference whether you start with your toes or your scalp. If you start at the bottom, focus all of your attention on your feet. You can wiggle your toes or squeeze them together to help you feel them. Then tell them to relax. Move up to the ankles, the calves, etc., until you get to your chin, mouth, nose, facial muscles, eyes, ears, forehead, and scalp. The more you practice, the more you'll be able to focus in on, and be aware of, each individual part of your body.

John Gray, in *How to Get What You Want and Want What You Have* (1999), describes a meditation process in which you hold your hands up, so they are not touching anything, and focus on one finger at a time (wiggling it slightly in the beginning to start the feeling), until you can actually feel energy move through the fingertip. Do this with each finger in order, and repeat until you've gone through all fingers ten times.

repeated in
p. 137

Another practice is to pay attention to and become more aware of your skin. Feel your clothes touching your body, feel the air or breeze on your skin as you walk, and when you're sitting, feel the chair or couch beneath you and your feet against the floor. When you're lying in bed, feel the covers against your skin and the softness of the pillow and the mattress under you. All of these exercises also help you to develop clarity and precision of focus.

# Chapter 25
# Grokking and Archetypes

> "Grok means chewing on a concept and assimilating it until it becomes one with you and your understanding rather than swallowing it whole and half-digested."
> – *Lama Surya Das*

The term "grok" was coined by Robert Heinlein in *Stranger in a Strange Land.* *Star Trek* fans are also familiar with this notion in the science fiction world. There is an exercise given in Serge King's Huna classes he calls grokking, which has also been practiced and utilized in many shaman traditions, though most probably don't use that term.

King explains in his class how shamans would meditate on a tree or animal and imagine their spirits merging with the spirit of the tree or animal, becoming one with it and assimilating its energy. When this is done, the shaman then has a deep understanding of what it is like to be that tree or animal from its own perspective and sometimes even senses images or memories of the particular energy's experience. The energy of a person (whether living, in the past, or imaginary), can also be grokked in the same way. You could grok someone who is charismatic by imagining that person in detail with all the characteristics you wish to develop, tuning in to that person's energy and charisma. Then imagine your spirit stepping into that person's body. Gain the feeling and understanding of what it would be like to be that person, in a fully associated state, as if you were looking through that person's eyes.

In *Awakening the Buddha Within* (1997), Lama Surya Das discusses visualizing yourself as a specific mystical deity in order to embody the qualities to which you aspire. He clarifies that it is less important to be able to visualize or graphically imagine the forms and attributes of the deity than it is to viscerally "feel" the presence of the invoked meditational deity, embodying the qualities you are learning to cultivate. However, Das explains, "There are no deities per se in Buddhism. Instead these numinous forms are archetypes embodying the most noble and sublime qualities we can aspire to achieve – more personifications of spiritual principles like wisdom, compassion, healing power, and so on." In this way, you can personify characteristics of charisma, creating an archetype. In Serge King's grokking exercise, you are also really working with archetypes in the form of someone you know, know of, or imagine.

Charismatic people have many admirable qualities and characteristics. Since we are naturally drawn to people who exhibit qualities we lack or admire, I believe part of the magnetism of charisma is that we recognize these qualities and characteristics that we would like to express more of ourselves. These exercises will help you to discover and develop these to a greater extent than you otherwise might.

Nijole Sparkis says of charismatic people, "In a way, they are no longer just a regular person, but they become an archetype – a mythical symbol for some characteristic of humanity. Somehow their character, presence and being represents a universal human characteristic so deeply, that it demands our attention. We recognize that there is something here for us, perhaps a message, perhaps something to learn or to take note of, sometimes even something to reject – something that contains a kernel of the essence of life."

In the videotape seminar *Rare Bandler* (1982), Richard Bandler discusses a process similar to grokking in order to program yourself to go toward a desired outcome, such as highly developing a skill. In one variation, this approach would consist of imagining a slide (or still image) of yourself and then running a movie from it, where the desired action is being done perfectly, first in a dissociated state (seeing yourself in the picture, rather than experiencing it in the first person). Then, step inside the movie to experience it in an associated state until you experience doing it perfectly. Bandler himself has used this strategy to develop his proficiency as a magician. He sees himself doing the trick flawlessly, then gets inside the movements on his mental screen, imagining himself doing it until he can perform the routine perfectly. In another variation, Bandler has also used this technique with martial arts, first seeing the teacher perfectly in his mind, then getting closer and closer, following the movements, eventually stepping inside the muscles and experiencing it as he himself doing the movements as the teacher did them.

# Chapter 26
# Expanding Energy

> "Charisma is a matter of expanding your sense of self to embrace all the people with whom you come in contact."
> – *Roger Dawson*

Intuitively, charisma seems to be connected to one's energy field and indicated by an expanded aura, which might also be described as an expanded sense of self. I have had the experience of knowing charismatic people who, without the use of any of the five physical senses, I can "feel" when they enter the room, when I am facing away. I can sense the intensity of their energy fields. When I turn around, they are there.

I had a voice teacher in college, Phyllis Murray, who used to instruct her students to "fill the room with your presence." She didn't explain what that meant or how to do it, but (presupposing that it could be done) I was able to tune in to and sense my own energy field and imagine it expanding to all the corners of the room.

Many celebrities are described as being "larger than life." Could this be an unconscious literal use of language (Chapter 21) to reflect an expanded energy field? Does this relate to internal representations and submodalities (Chapter 20)? Do charismatic people actually see certain internal images larger or hear internal voices louder or have more intense feelings? Is this the image of themselves that they project so that other people experience them in this way?

In a hypnotherapy conference I attended a few years back, one of the speakers used dowsing rods to measure how far each volunteer's aura came out from her body. She then had the volunteer close her eyes and whispered directions to either think about something that angered or upset the person or, conversely, to think of something that made the person feel blissful or strong. The other participants in the presentation did not know what the presenter whispered or what each person was thinking about. The presenter would then measure the person's aura again (while the person still had her eyes closed) before the volunteer was allowed to open her eyes and see the new dimensions of her aura. Invariably, when someone thought "negative" thoughts, the aura was collapsed compared to the "neutral" reading; with "positive" thoughts, the aura expanded to fill the room, and sometimes beyond. Your thoughts affect your energy field, as well as your physical body, as has been scientifically documented.

Another way to expand your energy is to first expand your awareness by what is known as the "learning state." I first learned about this state in classes taught by Gloria Ginn around 1990 for naturally improving physical vision. This process, where you open up your vision to include the entire room, later became an integral part of my hypnotherapy training, and it was reviewed in several degree-related classes I took.

The learning state is a light trance state that makes it easy to absorb information at an unconscious level and to retrieve it consciously. Since learning is state-related, during tests many students can't remember information previously learned because they're not in the same state they were in when they learned the information. This is also why during the night and thinking about a dream you had, still in a sleepy state, you're positive you'll still remember it in the morning. Being in a different state in the morning, you remember little, if any, of the dream.

To achieve the learning state, you want to completely relax, arms hanging loosely by your sides, while your head and spine are comfortably lifted, as if they were being held in place by a string from above. Pick a point in front of you on the wall to focus on, above eye level. I learned this state by picking a point where the wall meets the ceiling. If the ceiling is really high, however, you might want to pick a spot on the wall.

While your central vision is focusing on this single point, let your vision relax more and more, opening up your awareness of the periphery across the front of the room and seeing everyone and everything in front of you and to your sides. Gradually bring your eyes down, so you are looking straight ahead, while maintaining this awareness of your periphery in front, to either side, above, below, and even and have a sense of awareness behind you, as well, even though you won't be able to physically see behind you. Have the sense of being at one with the room, with no boundaries between you and other people or objects. See and feel everything as energy with all the atoms flowing together as a part of the whole, like individual drops of water that also comprise the ocean.

I remember a Christmas Eve in the Midwest when I was young, kneeling on my bed, looking out the window at the softly falling snow across the light of the street lamps and the blanket of snow across the neighbors' front yards. Even though I was looking out the limited space of a window, I remember the feeling of the entire night sky, snow falling all around the house, and what the entire neighborhood looked like at night, as if I could see it all clearly. The learning state is a natural state for children, as we learn so quickly and automatically when we're young. See if you have such a memory of that feeling state.

There are many exercises to experience and increase awareness of the energy in your body, aura strengthening, and energy building. I recommend the following resources, if you are interested in pursuing this further: Donna Eden's book *Energy Medicine* and her video series *Energy Healing*; Master Chunyi Lin's video and audio series *Spring Forest Qigong*; and Master Lam Kam Chuen's book *The Way of Energy*.

Continuing to develop your awareness of your energy and to expand your awareness of the energy around you will make it easier for you to influence the energy in your vicinity and to project your energy more powerfully, which you will learn more about later.

# Chapter 27
# Past/Present/Future

> "The past does not equal the future, unless you live there."
> – *Tony Robbins*

People who are charismatic do not allow their past to dictate their future. What is it that distinguishes the past from the future? The present. The present is a manifestation of past thoughts and actions. The future is a manifestation of the thoughts and actions of the present. Therefore, you can change the future by changing the present, which is all you can change anyway.

If you don't do anything different in the present, nothing will change, and the past will equal the future. However, you can change the future by changing your thoughts and actions right now.

Most people operate on automatic pilot, being ruled by habit. What is habit? Habit is when we consciously choose a particular thought or action consistently enough that it moves out of consciousness and into our unconscious. This is why habits are so difficult to break. They are no longer conscious. If we could change them on the conscious level, they wouldn't present any problem. That's where hypnosis presents a solution. It bypasses the conscious mind and communicates directly with the unconscious mind.

People who are charismatic give the impression that they are fearless. And, if you think about it, this makes sense. Fear can exist only in future thinking. Fear, worry, and anxiety are the anticipation of something that might happen in the future, even if it is in the immediate future. If you are focused in the present moment, however, fear cannot exist. But, this is not to say that fear doesn't have its place.

Fear is a legitimate emotion when in imminent physical danger and there is a need to react instinctually, without thought. When this is the case, you can remain in the flow, in the moment, and automatically react in whatever way is necessary to get you out of harm's way. However, when you dwell in fear, it is an ego-based emotion that cuts off your "flow" of energy and prevents you from being in the "now" or moving forward. This happens when there is a fear of losing what is already possessed or not attaining what is wanted or needed. In that case, you are stuck in your thoughts and not experiencing what you do have at that time. In a sense, you remove yourself from the present moment, as you are living in your thoughts of anxiety.

When I was organizing, goal-setting, and beginning this writing, I went to a chiropractor because of severe tension in my shoulders. I didn't tell him what I was doing, but when treating me, Dr. Dan Lechowicz mentioned that information is stored throughout the body, and that future programming is stored in the shoulders. This is usually mostly about work, but when I was thinking in future terms, my shoulders got tense. The best solution for my tension was to bring myself back to the present.

Dr. Jonny Bowden, in the Internet article, "Nine Things You Can Stop Worrying About," advises that there are three important things you should know about the past: it's over; you can't change it; and "the only thing keeping it alive is the energy you put into holding on to it." Describing how one of the most liberating events in your life can be letting go of the past, he further explains, "It means allowing what was to be what it was – and also, what it was not. It doesn't necessarily mean forgetting, but it does mean forgiving – both yourself and others."

The only problem with this is that often we don't even realize what we're holding onto or why. It's unconscious. We hold on out of habit. Also, there is a reason (conscious, unconscious, or both) why we don't let go of negative or unproductive thoughts about past events. Hypnosis can assist us in discovering the what, why, and how.

You might already have realized that you are who you are now because of everything that has happened to you before and because of your expectation of what will happen in the future. The only meaning the past and future have is in their relevance to "now." There are, of course, benefits to taking time periodically to review the past and to plan for future possibilities; but this is something that is done with purpose, not arbitrarily.

You can't change the past, although you can change your perception of the past, how you feel about the past, and reinterpret what you've gained from it. You can learn from the past, using it to guide you toward what you want and what you don't want, what works and what doesn't work. It got you to where you are, but the only way you can get someplace different is through the present. And you can.

✡ ✡ ✡

# Chapter 28
# Present Moment Awareness

> "In my seminars, I know I've captured the right rhythm when I am actually so present that I'm not consciously monitoring what I'm saying – I am just 'being' in the flow of speaking."
> – *Stephan Rechtschaffen*

In *Time Shifting* (1996), charismatic author/speaker Rechtschaffen continues, "At such times, I get the palpable feeling from my listeners that they're 'with' me just as I am 'with' them."

People who are charismatic give an impression of aliveness. You can achieve this only when you are fully focused in the present, tuned in to your environment, and aware of people, places, and events around you, with all five senses, as well as being aware of your own internal feelings and behavior, and the behavior of others. Being in the moment also opens up your intuition, because you are not distracted by idle thoughts. The more focused you are in the present, the more presence or charisma you will have.

You can imagine someone who is charismatic, can't you? It doesn't matter whether this is someone you know, a celebrity or public figure, or a fictional character such as James Bond or Xena, Warrior Princess. You can tell whether or not a person is present by looking into his or her eyes. The eyes of a charismatic person always sparkle with alertness and involvement. You have no doubt where this person's attention is. He or she is not distracted by rehashing the past or planning the future (as most people are most of the time), with the exception of times that the person sets aside specifically for that purpose.

The only time you have for demonstrating power is in the present moment. Therefore, it would make sense that you would have the highest level of personal power when you are fully in the present moment.

Hypnotherapy and other studies of the workings of the unconscious mind show that the unconscious mind is literal. It does not interpret the way the conscious mind does. Therefore, symbolic language, puns, metaphors, and other plays on words, are powerful tools in bypassing the analytical conscious mind and communicating directly with the subconscious. It is not coincidental that the terms "having presence" and "being present" come from the same root. In order to have presence, you must be completely present.

A charismatic politician or speaker will be poised and centered, able to field questions easily because her attention is focused on now, and not on remembering a speech (past thinking) or worrying about not being able to answer questions (future thinking). He or she knows the material and will be guided by the audience and current mood rather than by static memorized words. Motivational speakers and trainers learn to be "in rapport" with their audience by developing sensory acuity, or acute sensory perception, an awareness available only if they are very much in the present.

Comedians who are charismatic, like politicians, can respond to hecklers quickly and effectively. They can improvise only if they are in the moment and able to utilize everything at their disposal, which requires an acute awareness.

A charismatic singer will be experiencing the feeling contained in each word sung, while the singer's outer focus will be connecting with the audience, such that each person watching and listening will feel that the performer is singing directly to him or her. This singer makes eye contact throughout the audience and interacts with the audience's reactions. We can tell if a singer is focused on hitting the right notes or remembering the lyrics, or actually emoting the song with present feeling. We aren't moved by a song unless the singer is feeling what he or she is singing, which can happen only in present moment awareness.

Charismatic actors are always aware of their present surroundings. If they miss a line, another actor messes up a line, a prop doesn't work, or something else unexpected happens, they can easily adapt and react appropriately in character without getting flustered. Being in the moment also keeps lines sounding and reactions appearing fresh, night after night or take after take, as every moment is new, as if it is happening for the very first time. As with singers, being "in character" or expressing lines with appropriate feeling can only happen if the actor is "present."

Top martial artists have a commanding energy of charisma and presence. One of my theories is that martial artists (as well as gangsters, who are also often charismatic) have to be aware at all times of everything going on around them, as well as their feelings and intuition, because of possible physical threat. Martial artists must always be aware of every nuance of their surroundings, for their own physical safety. This sensitivity is an integral part of their training, with a fully developed sensory awareness and ability to react instantly and instinctively.

Dancers (who have acquired such physical sensitivity and agility that they can consciously control almost every muscle in their bodies) are always in the moment if they are to be in top form and exude presence and emotion. Acrobats, gymnasts, and other athletes must demand nothing less of themselves in order to be at the top of their game, to avoid injury, and to execute every move as perfectly as possible. Any accomplished athlete is always "in his or her body" and aware of any physical sensation. The best athletes are often thought of as being charismatic.

Yogis, shamans, and other spiritual leaders who teach us to live in the present moment and with total awareness are some of the most charismatic people who ever lived.

✫ ✫ ✫

# Chapter 29
# Procrastination

> "You are not stuck in life; you are stuck in what
> you've told yourself life is about."
> – *Guy Finley*

Even procrastination involves self-talk. When you
procrastinate, you identify with what you don't want, taking you
out of the present moment. When you are charismatic, you refuse
to "buy into" the negative thoughts and images that pop up,
unheralded. Instead, you identify with what you *do* want. There
is no struggle with what you don't want, as it holds no interest for
you. Therefore, these negativities have no power over you. The
only power or authority that any thoughts or feelings have over you
is the power you assign to them. When you are stuck in a thought
(including chastising yourself for procrastinating), you step out
of life's ever-changing flow and stop moving. Your attention and
energy are no longer in the constantly moving present, but in
being stuck.

Procrastination is one way the unconscious mind avoids
being present. When you are charismatic, you are "in the flow,"
and not stuck in the past, future, or the limbo of procrastination.
Instead of thinking of yourself as being a procrastinator, consider
that you use procrastination as a way of coping in some areas of
your life, as a solution to dealing with fears. This helps to remove
your identification with procrastinating as part of who you are. It's
easier to change a behavior or attitude than it is an identity.

In order to be charismatic, your energy has to be where you
are, in this moment, directed by you, in a way that's determined by

you. This appears obvious, but the reason you are somewhere else may not be so obvious.

Neil Fiore (*Conquering Procrastination*, 1995) identifies the five phrases that guarantee procrastination: "I have to," "finish," "something big and very important," "do it perfectly," and then "spend lots of time in pain and deprivation." He suggests changing your language this way: "I have to" to "I choose to"; "finish" to "start"; "something big and very important" to "one small step"; "do it perfectly" to "do it humanly"; and "spend lots of time in pain and deprivation" to "with plenty of time for living now and plenty of guilt-free play on my schedule." The new statement now reads, "I choose to start one small step, do it humanly, with plenty of time for living now and plenty of guilt-free play on my schedule." Doesn't that have a freeing feeling to it?

David Allen's two-day seminar recording *Getting Things Done. . . Fast: The Ultimate Stress-Free Productivity System* (2001) discusses how to handle procrastination that stems from feeling overwhelmed. "The reason something is on your mind is not because it's unfinished, it's because either the outcome has not been clarified, the next action has not been defined, or you have not parked reminders of those outcomes or actions in a place your brain trusts you will see at the right time." When you've made an internal commitment about something, either psychologically or physically, but haven't clarified what it is or organized it, that's when you feel the pressure and anxiety. You might feel overwhelmed by the big picture of large projects, rather than seeing the immediate next step in front of you. This can keep you stuck, unable to move anywhere.

Allen goes so far as to say, "Until your mind trusts that there is a system better than it is to remember and remind, it cannot let it go." Although your unconscious mind always remembers everything, the mind keeps what it thinks you need to be consciously reminded of in what Allen refers to as "psychic RAM," which is highly inefficient. What you have not dealt with, or devised a way of dealing with, will constantly distract you.

Also, we are often so habituated to doing several things at once, that slowing down enough to experience the present moment becomes stressful, and we have the feeling that we have to hurry and be productive every moment, with the nagging worry that we should be doing something else. This mentally disorganized consciousness makes life an open loop, where we don't know how much we have left to do, so we're always concerned about getting everything done.

A beginning technique for dealing with the situation of having an overfilled mind is to perform what David Allen refers to as a complete "mind sweep." As a preliminary step, take a pad of paper and go through every inch of your home and workplace environments, writing down everything you see that represents a project or a task.

Next, the "mind sweep" is where you write down everything that is on your mind that you would like to do or might like to do, regardless of your level of commitment to doing it or how realistic it is. If anything is left on your mind at all without being written down, it will distract you. Now you have clarified all the outcomes. This is not a static list, by the way. Continue to add to it any time you think of anything else.

After clarifying outcomes, the next step is defining next actions, by making various lists: first of projects (anything requiring more than one step), depending upon your level of commitment; then list each task, based on location, such as "At Computer," "At Home," "Phone Calls," "Errands," etc. Decide what you need to do next for each project, making sure there is an entry on one of the "location" lists for it.

To put your mind at ease that nothing will be missed, sit down and review your lists at least once a week. Update them, removing anything you've completed and adding any new tasks that come to mind. Make sure that you still have a "next action" for each project. Now your mind is released from feeling overwhelmed and free to be present.

Procrastination can also occur when you feel a threat to your self-worth. In beginning a process of change, you need to identify the words, feelings, and images associated with procrastination, and be ready with alternatives that shift your attention to effective, goal-oriented actions when procrastination appears.

# Chapter 30
# Calling Your Spirit Back

> "Our spirits, our energy, and our personal power are all one and the same force."
> – *Caroline Myss*

Sometimes you are not in the present moment because you have too many things on your mind. However, it could also be that your mind is in more than one place and/or time. If your thoughts are anywhere other than where you are, your energy is scattered, as thoughts are energy. You need to be aware of how and what you are thinking so you know what to change in your thought patterns to increase your presence and charisma.

Most people have their energy fragmented, with their minds drifting between several different places in space and time. If your focus is on a disempowering emotion, circumstance, or person, you "lose" that "energy" that you've vested your attention in – the energy will be "flowing" to the past or the future and/or different locations, not the here and now. When energy is scattered, you cannot be fully present. The more fully you are in the present moment, the less your energy will be fragmented. The more energy you have focused where you are right now, the more energy you will have access to, which gives you a more powerful appearance of intense magnetism.

I believe that when you lack charisma, you have in some way detached from a connection with your "spirit," or energy source. As in the next story, you have left parts of your spirit with past (or even future anticipated) experiences or feelings that disconnect you from your present self.

A dramatic example is from Caroline Myss' *Anatomy of the Spirit* (1996), in which she discusses the Navajo Indian practice of "calling back the spirit." When they recognize that they've given part of their "spirit" (i. e., attention, power, or energy) away, they can then make a conscious new decision so that they can be more fully present and empowered.

Navajo Indian David Chetlahe Paladin was in the U. S. military in the 1940s and was captured and tortured by Nazis. After the war, he spent two and a half years in a coma in a military hospital, his body so weakened from his prison camp experiences that he could not walk after regaining consciousness. He was fitted for heavy leg braces and, using crutches, he could drag himself short distances. When David returned to his reservation to say a last good-bye to his people before entering a veterans' hospital, his family and friends gathered together to figure out how to help him. After holding a council meeting, the elders took the braces off of David's legs, tied a rope around his waist, and threw him into deep water, commanding him to call back his spirit.

Paladin told Myss that calling his spirit back was the most difficult task he ever had to undertake. He recounted having to endure having his feet nailed to the floor, and saw the faces of the Nazi soldiers, living through all those months in the prison camp. Barely able to keep himself from drowning, he knew he had to release his anger and hatred, and prayed to let the anger out of his body. His prayers were answered.

Having survived and transcended a confrontation with the darkest side of power, Paladin recovered the full use of his legs and went on to become a shaman, a Christian minister, and a healer, spending the rest of his life healing and inspiring people to "call back their power" from experiences that drain the life force from their bodies.

Myss summarizes, "we can retrieve our spirits from the false gods of fear, anger, and attachments to the past. Every attachment we hold on to out of fear commands a circuit of our spirit to leave our energy field."

When your energy is fragmented, or you notice yourself thinking negatively, it might be a good idea to ask yourself if what you're thinking about deserves your energy. If it does, remember the power of focusing on solutions, rather than problems, and how to ask yourself better questions that will make your focus more effective. If it is not worth your energy, you can "call back your spirit."

When in a meditative or hypnotic state, you can simply suggest to yourself that you are calling back all of your energy from wherever it may be. You can make up a self-guided meditation or visualization to represent this procedure, however it feels right to you. As an example, you can imagine yourself in a control tower, communicating with each part of you that you feel separated from, and then guide each part back to where it should be. As in the story of David Chetlahe Paladin, you may need to release some highly charged emotions before you can call all of your power back. Know that you can trust your unconscious mind to know what needs to be done and to come up with a way to do it.

✿ ✿ ✿

# Chapter 31
# Self-Integration

> "When someone…feels driven to do something he doesn't consciously want to do, we assume that an 'unconscious part' makes him do it."
> — *Connirae and Steve Andreas*

Most people are conflicted by different "parts" of themselves. We'll say, "Part of me wants to do this, while another part of me wants to do that." Procrastination is even described by Neil Fiore (*Conquering Procrastination*, 1995) as a tug of war between two parts of us, an inner six-year-old speaking in "have tos" to an inner three-year-old who doesn't want to "have to," who wants to do what he or she wants to do and not be told what to do. To get these two inner children to work together peacefully and efficiently, there are various processes we can call "parts therapy," "parts integration," or "self-integration."

These processes can be used if, for example, you want to be charismatic, but a part of you feels in conflict with this goal. It is important to separate intention from behavior. Any problem behavior you have has a positive purpose for you, although this purpose is usually unconscious. This behavior was, when it began, your solution to dealing with a particular issue or situation. When the positive purpose behind it is brought to conscious awareness, you can then choose a more productive behavior (either consciously or unconsciously) to achieve both the original purpose and the current result you want.

One process is to hold both your hands out in front of you, palms up. Imagine the "problem" part appearing on one of your hands. Get a visual and auditory sense of how that "part"

→ New option generator ←

represents itself to you. Mentally ask this part "for what purpose" does it not want you to be charismatic. Ask it to tell you what its highest intention is for you by preventing you from being charismatic. Keep asking "for what purpose" until you get an answer that is a genuine benefit, which you feel is at the root of the issue. Don't try to rationalize. Just ask and wait for an answer to pop into your mind. If nothing comes, then make something up (again, without rationalizing). There may be resistance to the answer, so pretending that you are making it up will usually get past the resistance. When you have a beneficial answer, realize that you agree with the positive purpose, even if you don't like the behavior or the results it actually gets for you.

Then ask the part that wants to be charismatic to come out on your other hand, get a visual and auditory sense of *this* "part," and elicit *its* highest intention for you. Make sure that the intention makes you the "actor," rather than being "acted upon." For instance, if the part says it "wants other people to like me," that puts the action outside of yourself (it's up to other people; you have no control). Reword it to perhaps, "have good relationships with others." When you are the one responsible for taking action, this gives you the power. This is just an example, and is not to imply that this will be the reason.

When you reach the highest intention for both parts, acknowledge the usefulness of both intentions. When you get right down to the root, you will likely find that the intentions of both are either identical or complementary to each other. Isn't that interesting? Realize that these two parts are in conflict only if you think of them as being in opposition. However, you can now see that they can be mutually supportive of each other. Ask each part if it already has a sense of how the other part can be useful to it.

Connirae and Steve Andreas describe the next step in *Heart of the Mind* (1989): "Then allow both your hands to slowly come together, only as fast as these two parts can blend together, keeping the important useful purposes of each, joining together in such a way that each benefits from the other, and loses nothing. You may be surprised by exactly how they change and merge when your hands come together, so I want you to take all the time you need for these parts to integrate at their own rate of speed." The process is completed by bringing your hands in to your chest, symbolically integrating the new part into your being. Both original parts are transformed and merged into one, to the benefit of the whole, prompting new responses and behaviors on an unconscious level.

There are numerous ways to work with parts, limited only by your imagination. If you have a "rebellious" part that is causing conflict, you can go through another process sometimes called a "parts intervention." You can begin by imagining a meeting room. See every detail of the room: the walls, ceiling, floor, any windows or doors, the table, and six chairs around the table. Six different "parts" will come through the door one at a time – the first two being positive parts, the next two neutral parts, then the rebellious part, and, lastly, a "magical" part. However these parts come to you and represent themselves is exactly right for this time. As each part enters, find out everything you can about it (ask what it would like to be called, notice if it has a gender, ask what it represents to you, etc. ), and ask it to take a seat. With each subsequent part, ask it if it knows the other part(s) in the room and, if not, introduce them to each other. This is usually done by a therapist, who draws a chart, writing down information on the setup of the room, each part, and where each part sits at the table. If you are by yourself, and you want to keep notes, you may record the information on the room, each part, and anything any of the parts tell you during the process.

When the meeting begins, find out exactly what upsets the rebellious part and what it is that it needs in order to feel taken care of and secure. Bring all the other parts into the discussion to come up with various solutions. If you get stuck, the "magical" part has a solution for everything, so ask the magical part for assistance.

Make sure that the rebellious part has a solution it is satisfied with, that meets its needs and concerns, and is agreeable to all the other parts. Before adjourning the meeting, go around the table and find out if any of the other parts have any issues they wish to be discussed or resolved. Once every point has been addressed, the parts can each say their good-byes and leave the room one at a time.

All of these processes engage the unconscious mind, using its own symbolic language. Since the problem is at the unconscious level, that's where you will find the solution.

# Chapter 32
# Spirituality and Charisma

> "Tibetan Buddhism says that at the heart of you,
> me, every single person…is an inner radiance that
> reflects our essential nature. . ."
> – *Lama Surya Das*

Tibetans call this inner light of pure radiance *ground luminosity* because it is "bottom line." I believe that this is the true origin of all charisma. How and if it is accessed and utilized is up to the individual. Although not specifically referred to as charisma, this concept of universality and having a basis within the spirit is also found in other cultures.

Entertainer Nijole Sparkis asserts, "Ultimately, the state of charisma is a kind of state of unity with the divine wholeness of which each of us is a part. The more we develop within ourselves this state of wholeness and unity with divine energies or ultimate purpose or utter faith, the more charismatic and attractive and magnetic we are."

Until the early twentieth century when German sociologist Max Weber used the term to describe powerful political figures with strong personalities, the term "charisma" had a religious connotation. The Greeks first used the word charisma to mean "a divine gift," followed by the Christian Church, which used the term similarly to describe attributes bestowed by God, such as wisdom, prophecy, or healing.

In today's vernacular, charisma is used in an even broader context to include entertainers, athletes, and anyone who exudes a powerful presence. Although the implication appears to have always been that those with charisma were different from ordinary people, I speculate that charisma, whatever one's interpretation might be, is a "gift" of the spirit that we are all born with, although some people access it more naturally than others, often as a result of their social environment and upbringing. I'm convinced that charisma is an outer expression of energy, or inner power, available to everyone. If you do not connect with it, or plug into it, it remains dormant, but it is still there to be tapped into.

Doe Lang, in 1999's *The New Secrets of Charisma*, considers that "charisma is a basic energy force of nature, like fire or water. It's value-free: it can be either positive or destructive, life-enhancing or imprisoning." She goes on to quote Greek poet Evangelos Alexandreou, who calls charisma the "jewelry of the human soul."

People who are charismatic have a great deal of personal power, but I don't think this power comes from communication, although it can be communicated. Charisma is, in fact, an energy that comes from within (i. e., it is perceived intuitively, or on a feeling level, rather than through any of the five physical senses), from the core of a person. By "core," I am referring to the non-visible part of every human being that we are all born with, that is present throughout our existence, and does not change. The core contains elements that are common to all humans. How we communicate, on the other hand, is a learned behavior (usually adopted unconsciously by example of those around us), which may reinforce or separate us from our natural charisma.

Charisma can be enhanced by developing communication skills and the ability to influence others. I realized this when I thought about someone who is intelligent and well-educated. At first the two seem to go together; however, if we think about it, we recognize that there are many intelligent people who are not formally well-educated, as well as people who are well-educated who don't exhibit a whole lot of intelligence. Again, intelligence is something inherently at the core of a person, and (school-based or self-taught) education is learning that can enhance naturally occurring intelligence, though some people mistake one for the other. I believe that we all have intelligence and charisma at our core. Some people access one or both naturally or by conscious decision. Others neglect to tap into them at all. And still others, because of the environment they grew up in, were "taught" that they didn't have a right to these characteristics, didn't possess them, or that they had to be worked at to be achieved, and thus lost touch with these inner gifts they started out with.

# Chapter 33
# The Importance of Breathing

"Every brain state, every emotional state, has a corresponding brainwave pattern and breath pattern...If you adopt the breathing pattern of a relaxed person, you literally fool the body...into thinking it's relaxed."
– *Marc David*

What does breathing have to do with charisma? Since charisma is a state, it therefore has a corresponding brainwave pattern and breath pattern, part of the physiology of charisma. Some of the most charismatic people – singers, actors, dancers, martial artists, yogis, and shamans – are all trained in breathing techniques, habitually breathing fully and regularly. This optimizes oxygen intake, which feeds the body, mind, emotions, and spirit.

Conscious breathing brings your awareness to the present moment. Of course, you can't breathe consciously all the time, but from time to time you can bring your awareness to your breathing to reset your internal clock, slow down your thoughts, become more relaxed, and bring you back to now. Both hypnosis and meditation typically use breathing as a way to focus attention and awareness in one place. In martial arts and yoga, breathing is a discipline in itself. It is the source of mental and physical power.

Most of us don't get enough oxygen. Yes, we get enough to keep us alive, but not enough for us to operate at our optimum, physically, mentally, emotionally, and maybe even spiritually. In our hectic lives, we tend to unconsciously hold our breath, especially under stress, as if trying to stop time and fit more into the time we have. In our society, we also tend to be shallow breathers, as well as breathing irregularly. Oxygen assists all physical functions, including metabolism and elimination. Medically, oxygen treatments are generally the last resort to keeping someone alive. Proper breathing improves health and weight management, which then improves self-esteem and confidence. I've known overweight people who were charismatic, but they tend to be the exception, not the rule.

Oxygen also improves mental functioning and alertness, promotes physical and mental relaxation, and balances the emotions, making it easier to manage your states or feelings. Since you have to breathe anyway, once you learn and practice breathing properly and fully, it doesn't take any extra time, just an occasional shift of attention.

In *Time Shifting* (1996), Stephan Rechtschaffen asserts that breathing is one of the simplest and most effective ways to become present in your life. "Breathing is a way of bringing us mentally and emotionally back to center...By allowing ourselves to become conscious of our breathing, we begin to slow down into the breath and allow ourselves to set a rhythm for the body that is peaceful, calm, and healthy." This is one way that charismatic people attain their characteristic calm, yet intense, demeanor.

Jon Kabat-Zinn contends that a good way to nurture mindfulness is to tune in to the feeling of your breathing. In *Wherever You Go, There You Are* (1994), Kabat-Zinn instructs you to become aware of the feeling of the breath coming into your body and the feeling of the breath leaving your body. "Breathing and knowing that you are breathing. This doesn't mean deep breathing or forcing your breathing, or trying to feel something special, or wondering whether you are doing it right." Simply be aware.

Thich Nhat Hanh (*The Present Moment*, 1994) informs his listeners that smiling relaxes the face and nervous system. He instructs them to say to themselves, while breathing, "Breathing in, smile; breathing out, release, let go." Hanh observes that most of us live in the state of habit, being alive, but not being aware that we are alive. Most of his teaching is to be aware of what you are doing. When you eat, be aware that you are eating by consciously looking at, smelling (when appropriate, touching), and tasting the food. When you are walking, be aware of each time one of your feet touches the ground.

Breathing deeply and fully is natural to infants, but we lose that instinct quickly and our shallow breathing becomes a habit most of our lives, for most people. To regain the feeling of breathing naturally, exhale completely until you push every last drop of air out of your lungs, pressing your stomach inward. Wait for a few moments, then allow the air to rush back into your lungs. Your body will breathe instinctively, filling the lungs up fully. The more you practice this exercise, the more accustomed you will become to breathing fully and increasing your supply of oxygen. To allow your lungs to expand even more, you can raise your arms above your head, then drop them as you bend over forward and exhale completely. Raise your arms and body, stretching up on the inhale.

You tend to breathe more naturally and deeply when you sleep, regenerating and reinvigorating your cells. Also, your physiology, including breathing, changes when your state changes. For instance, remember a time when you felt in love or that feeling of being physically attracted to someone. Fully associate to that state, so that you are experiencing it right now. If you were coming from a different state, you probably noticed that you changed your posture in order to accomplish this state, and that your breathing automatically became fuller.

As for spiritually, there may be a deeper meaning to the biblical statement that God breathed into man's nostrils the breath of life, and man became a living soul. Maybe there is a literal connection between breath and the soul. We can live for weeks without food, days without water, but not more than a few minutes without breathing. When we stop breathing, we die. When breath leaves the body, perhaps that's the soul leaving.

For an energy exercise, lie still and focus on your breath until you can feel the breath moving throughout your entire body, not just your lungs. Feel every part and every cell of your body as you breathe. After a while, it feels as if your body starts breathing you, and you are merely an observer. The oxygen sparks every cell, infusing them with energy and you can actually feel the cells vibrating and feel their individual life. You start to experience your entire body as energy, pure energy, which is what it is, after all: spirit in physical form. And, charisma is the energy of your spirit.

# Chapter 34
# Meditation as a Pathway

"Regular meditation assists you in reconnecting to the aspect of your inner self that is connected to God."
– *John Gray*

You probably realize meditation's benefits for stress reduction, slowing down the breathing and heart rate, lowering blood pressure, and relaxing the mind and body. But, how does this relate to charisma?

Meditation also brings you into the present. Meditation is actually the same state as hypnosis, but has a different function. With hypnosis, you typically enter the state for the purpose of working on a particular issue. However, you can use meditation to clear your mind of all the "chatter" by allowing all the thoughts about the past and the future to just float by you without analyzing or judging them. You keep thoughts stuck by rehashing them. If you just watch your thoughts without mentally grasping at them, most of them will sort themselves out and drift away without any rationalization or conscious effort. Using this process, creative ideas will often come to you, as well as solutions to problems you were not even thinking about. You can also meditate with the intention of tuning in to a solution to a particular problem and letting it float to you from wherever you think it might be – your unconscious mind, your higher self, your spirit guides, etc.

Another way to meditate, which brings you into the present and dissipates chatter, is to sit or lie with your eyes closed, and focus on your breathing. To prevent a rush of thoughts, you can either also focus on a "mantra" (sacred word or sound), such as "ommm" or "one," or an affirmation of your choosing. Although "ommm" and other mantras may have a particular beneficial energy frequency, they also focus your mind in one place.

You can also focus on *how* you breathe. In the Polynesian culture, there is a breathing method called "piko-piko." Piko (pronounced pee´-koh) means center. The Polynesians, as well as many cultures and disciplines, consider the energy body to have two centers – the crown, or top, of the head and the solar plexus (also known as the third chakra, tan tien, seat of power where we store energy, and the enteric nervous system). The solar plexus is where we have "gut feelings," and is also known as "the brain of the belly." According to Marc David (*Mind/Body Nutrition*, 2006), it has a "rich and complicated network of neurons and neurochemicals that sense and control events in the digestive tract and can sense events in other parts of the body, including your brain, including your experience of food. You might think that it's your head brain that's telling everything what to do, but, in reality, it's the gut that's in control, that's feeding the brain information, that's really the catalog, the encyclopedia, the warehouse of all the nutritional and digestive information in your body."

Piko-piko breathing focuses attention first on the crown of the head, while breathing in, then mentally following the exhale along an imaginary column from the crown down to the solar plexus. On the inhale, follow this column back from the solar plexus up to the crown. Continue this throughout the meditation. You can even imagine this column extended down into the earth, and out the crown of your head, going up to the heavens.

Another way you can use your breathing to focus your attention is to inhale to a slow count of six, hold your breath for a count of six, exhale for a count of six, and again hold your breath for a count of six. This requires all of your attention, circumventing chatter.

When you meditate, your posture is also important. Jon Kabat-Zinn, in *Wherever You Go, There You Are* (1994), tells us that our posture talks to us, making its own statement. It can also be the meditation itself. Slumping reflects low energy, passivity, or a lack of clarity. Sitting ramrod straight, causes tension and shows that you are making too much of an effort, trying too hard. In teaching situations, Kabat-Zinn advises his students to sit in a way that embodies dignity. Everybody's posture immediately adjusts to sit up straighter, but not stiffen. Kabat-Zinn describes the effect: "Faces relax, shoulders drop, head, neck, and back come into easy alignment. The spine rises out of the pelvis with energy." This is the correct posture of meditation and also embodies charisma.

Kabat-Zinn goes on to ask his readers to sit with dignity for thirty seconds, noting how they feel. Then he asks them to stand with dignity, being aware of where their shoulders, spines, and heads are. What would it mean to walk with dignity? He also finds it helpful in teaching for his students to hold the image of a mountain for deepening concentration and mindfulness in the sitting practice. "Invoking qualities of elevation, massiveness, majesty, unmovingness, rootedness, helps bring these qualities directly into posture and attitude." It is important to invite and practice the qualities of dignity, stillness, and unwavering equanimity, which can provide a solid, reliable foundation for maintaining mindfulness and emotional balance, even in periods of extreme stress and emotional turmoil. These are also qualities that are helpful in cultivating charisma.

John Gray (*How to Get What You Want and Want What You Have*, 1999) offers an advanced meditation process he learned when he was a monk, living in the mountains of Switzerland. Begin by closing your eyes and reaching your hands up in the air a little above shoulder height, or wherever it is comfortable. Focus on one fingertip at a time, wiggling the finger slightly to get a feeling of it, and then imagining energy flowing into the fingertip. In his religious setting, he also repeats the phrase, "Oh, God, my heart is open to you, please come sit in my heart." You may decide to use that sentiment or another sentiment that invokes a connection with your spiritual, energy side. This process is repeated with each fingertip, with the intention to awaken and open the channels of energy in that fingertip. With practice, you will gradually develop a tingling feeling in each finger as you do this, increasing an awareness of the subtle energy flow.

This awareness can then be extended beyond the meditation period and expanded throughout your body, increasing your feeling of charisma.

# Chapter 35
# The Stage Fright Project

> "When I used to coach singing clients on how to overcome self-doubt or stage fright, I would simply have them switch their focus away from their personal feelings about themselves and how they are doing, and onto...the interpretation of the song."
> – *Nijole Sparkis*

When I was in undergraduate school in Colorado, I did a term project on stage fright. I sent out questionnaires to around two hundred singers, musicians, and actors around the country (some were professional, but most were not), whom I considered to be excellent performers. I asked them if they ever experience stage fright, how it affects them, and what they do to overcome it. Although a handful did not experience stage fright, the vast majority did, at least at certain times.

The ways that these artists handled stage fright were quite varied, from deep breathing exercises, to pacing, to aerobics, to yoga or meditation, to whistling, to doing headstands or cartwheels. Thinking about it, taking into account what I know now, the one thing that all these "techniques" have in common is that they all brought the person back to the present moment. None of them expressed it in that way. Stage fright, by definition, is based on fear. People are afraid of forgetting the words or the chords, missing a note, tripping, or otherwise embarrassing themselves in some way in front of an audience. Fear is always of something that is in the future, that may or may not happen. When we bring ourselves back to the present moment, there is no fear or anxiety.

It is very common for an artist to say that once he is onstage or once she starts performing, the stage fright goes away. This could be explained in that the artist's focus shifts from possible mishaps to the audience, the music, or the role.

Nijole Sparkis, quoted at the beginning of this chapter, continues to say that she would have her clients focus on the meaning of the lyrics and becoming the character that is telling the story of that song. She explains, "The state of 'being' is the divine state, rather than the state of 'thinking' or the state of 'acting.' When a performer is thinking about how they are doing, everyone in the audience thinks about how that performer is doing. There is a disconnect from the wholeness of the divine experience. The experience becomes divine when everyone, the performer and the audience both, take the emotional ride that the song has been crafted to evoke. That is when audiences find the performer irresistibly charismatic."

In addition to focus, stage fright also ties into the previously covered concepts of interpretation and language. In *Unleash the Power Within* (1999), Tony Robbins relays the physical sensations of two artists before they go on stage and what it means to each of them. Carly Simon couldn't go on stage because of her extreme stage fright. Bruce Springsteen, on the other hand, couldn't wait to get on stage. Robbins relates that Carly Simon describes her symptoms this way, "When I think about going on stage, what happens is, my heart starts beating really, really fast, and my muscles in my hands start to tighten up and I start to sweat, and my breathing starts to speed up, and I think about going out there and everything starts speeding up faster and faster. I feel all this tension and all this pressure, and then I know I'm having a panic attack and I can't go out."

Bruce Springsteen, according to Robbins, conveys his experience in a similar manner, but with a different interpretation: "You know, when I think about going out there, everything in my body starts speeding up. I feel this tension in my hands and I start sweating. Still today, just like before, my heart starts beating like crazy, and right then, I know I'm ready."

Robbins summarizes, "Stressed and excited are very close – you put the language on it and it could go either way. Maybe you're not breaking down; maybe you're breaking through."

The feelings of adrenalin that Carly interprets as stage fright and anxiety, could be reframed to mirror Bruce's interpretation as excitement and anticipation. The bottom line to managing stage fright is what you focus on, what you believe about it, and staying in the present moment.

# Chapter 36
# Connection vs. Attachment

"Fritz Perls, the father of Gestalt psychology, coined the somewhat paradoxical phrase 'trying fails, awareness cures' to make the point that the harder we try, the more confused things often become, and that the remedy for 'trying too hard' is to be found in simple awareness."

– *Barry Green*

Yoda, of *Star Wars* fame, similarly states that there is no "try," only "do." Obi-Wan's lesson in connecting with The Force was one of simple and pure awareness, not effort. The paradox extends to the fact that you can only become connected to the charismatic state when you are not attached (e. g., trying) to achieving it. When you try to do something, there is some doubt that you can do it. Otherwise, you would just do it. And, when you do something successfully, you are not trying.

You only try when you are "attached" to the results or to what other people think. There is a definite magnetic quality to not being attached to what other people think and to not being attached to circumstances having to be a certain way in order to be comfortable. Our attachments include being stuck in our own thoughts and attitudes without flexibility to adapt when appropriate.

The concept of awareness versus trying or connection versus attachment is a clue to why most charismatic people are not aware of what charisma is or how it is created. At first this may not make sense relating to the rest of this book, but stay with me here and you'll see that it can explain how charisma can be both naturally occurring and developed.

Singer/entertainer Kyle Vincent told me in an interview, "I think if one has to put much thought into charisma, it's going to elude them…It's just there, as if I have little say in whether or not it displays itself." He may not have realized the correlation between this concept and a quote he gave in an online interview with "Popdose" (a music Web site). In "Popdose," he referred to being a shy teen. His voice was developing, but he hadn't brought it out yet. His voice teacher told him, "It's there, but you have to forget all of the stuff that's keeping it from coming out." It's the same with charisma. It's there, but you have to forget the stuff that's keeping it from coming out. Stop trying and just be there.

Some people do this naturally, both in singing and in charisma. Some people have a natural singing voice without any training, but most people have to train in order to develop a pleasant singing voice. Similarly, some people are naturally charismatic without knowing how they do it. However, most people need to learn "the basics" in order to be charismatic. Once the basics are learned, both in singing and in charisma, success is achieved only when your unconscious mind takes over and you consciously forget about what you're doing. "Training" in charisma is a fairly new concept though.

In my interview with Vincent, also an accomplished and prolific songwriter, he mentioned an interview he did for a book on artists and how they create. "My path is to completely forget about creating. When a procrastinating musician friend of mine asked me how best to write a song, I answered him with just four words: 'Write a damn song.'" Do you see a pattern developing here? When you are connected to the appropriate state, whether it's charisma or your creative side, you are doing and not thinking about how. Many of Vincent's best songs are the ones that were the easiest and fastest for him to write. He already knew how to write a great song. When he "forgot the stuff" required of a good song, he got out of his way and the songs materialized seemingly on their own.

Vincent's grandmother, a gifted artist, was able to let go of attachments in her later years. He said of her, "My grandmother did her best painting in her late seventies. I believe it corresponded to when she finally started to not really give a damn what anyone thought, or if anyone bought her works." Abraham Maslow, who coined the term "self-actualized," says that people who are self-actualized are "independent of the good opinions of others." This also applies to those who are charismatic. People who are charismatic work toward a purpose or intention, being focused on a direction (growth or improvement in a specific area), a process rather than a static end result.

I have a favorite story in Barry Green's *The Inner Game of Music* (1986). Green told of a cello student of his who had great difficulty executing a particular passage of music, even though it was within her capabilities. He asked her to demonstrate for the class how she was having trouble with the passage. When she was given permission to make a mistake, she was unable to recreate the error. Green explains, "The reason is simple. You have released yourself from the fear of failure and are now able to focus your attention one hundred percent on making music." When her focus shifted from trying to awareness, she allowed herself to become a part of the music. Permission to fail leads to success. This is another way of being in the moment and of not being attached to an end result.

Attachment is not only detrimental to performers and artists. In *Dick Clark's Program for Success* (1980), Clark describes how he periodically detaches from problems by visualizing a mental helicopter ride, getting a clearer view of his life and career. "I have never yet gotten trapped in a dead end, despite all my life and career crises, because I am always able to get away from myself, look at my situation from far above, and see the jams before I get stuck in any. Or, if trapped in one, my mental helicopter tells me which detour will get me out of the trap most quickly." He can connect to his intuition this way.

Entertainer Nijole Sparkis started acting when she was four years old, continuing into her teen years until she switched to singing. She loved the feeling of manipulating the emotions of the audience, making them feel whatever she expressed. When a struggling actor friend of hers was having a bout of insecurity and asked her how to get beyond stage fright, she was at a loss. Audiences loved her as a child actor and she internalized this experience to where, "I never thought people wouldn't like me. I never thought I'd fail!" She believes this feeling expresses "a performer's state of charisma." It also demonstrates how she makes a connection without being "attached" or afraid of failure.

# Chapter 37
# Sense of Purpose

> "You're here. Therefore, there's a purpose."
> *– Serge King*

I have never seen a charismatic person who didn't have a definite sense of purpose and inner knowing of what his or her place was in the scheme of life and the universe.

When people are charismatic, they appear to be on a mission. The great majority of charismatic people have a distinct sense of purpose. If they do not have an overall sense of purpose, they at least have some specific intention (but not attachment) for a definite outcome or direction. Although most people who are charismatic can articulate a specific purpose or intention, the importance is that they have a *sense* that there is a purpose to what they are doing, whether or not they can articulate that purpose.

Charismatic people know they belong here and they know where they fit into the scheme of things. This applies to a cult leader and a Hitler, as well as a John F. Kennedy or Barack Obama, a Mother Teresa, or a Rudolph Valentino. All charismatic people feel a certain "calling," a reason for being here, and they have goals that are meaningful for them.

Notice that I didn't say that charismatic people have a purpose, but that they have a *sense* of purpose. In *The Most Important Thing* (1988), Serge King explains that the feeling is what is important. "The feeling that you are fulfilling a purpose – *not fulfilling* a purpose,' cause each one of you are – *a feeling* that you are. That's different." If we don't have the awareness of fulfilling a purpose, the fact that we *are* fulfilling one doesn't matter to us.

Most people who are not charismatic don't consider or sense that they have a purpose.

In describing "right livelihood," Marsha Sinetar (*Do What You Love, The Money Will Follow*, 1987) says that if you live your life's purpose, your life's work is a mirror of yourself and something connected to yourself, a part of your spirit, mind, body, and senses. It also makes sense to your life in a synergistic context. Those who live with a sense of purpose, speak of their work in a way that indicates that they are at one with it. In my interview with entertainer Kyle Vincent, he says of songwriting, "It's what I need to do to survive. I must create."

Maybe it never occurred to you that you have a purpose or to think of yourself with a purpose. At this stage, you don't have to know what your purpose is, just decide that you have a purpose and experience internalizing the feeling of what it would be like to have a purpose. Serge King finds that an interesting thing will happen. "Once you can decide on, and grasp, and hold the feeling that you are fulfilling a purpose – surprise, surprise – one of these clear days, you'll find yourself doing something and loving it and knowing that that's your purpose. That's how it works…But some point along the way you have to make that decision, 'I am fulfilling a purpose.'"

You may not think you know how to find your purpose. You may be confused because you are doing what other people think you should be doing or doing what you think society expects from you or says is an honorable purpose. But, if it isn't who you really are, you intuitively know something's not quite right. You may even think you're lazy or something's wrong with you when you aren't happy in a successful or compassionate career that is someone else's purpose. But, it might just be resistance. You may tell yourself (over and over until you believe it) that you don't know what your purpose is in order to avoid facing your doubts and fears.

# Chapter 37: Sense of Purpose

In *How to Live the Life You Love* (1996), Barbara Sher tells us, "When our dreams are under too much siege in our early years, we hide them. And then what happens is we grow up and we forget where we hid them. But, they're waiting for you." You may also not think that what you really love can be your purpose. But it is. Sher states that there are no exceptions; what you love shows you what you're gifted at. Desire is your compass that points to your talent.

Regarding aptitude tests, Marsha Sinetar says, "No test can identify what is in our hearts to accomplish with our lives." Sinetar notes that you can find your purpose by using self-observation and memories. She suggests keeping a running list for a week or so of answers to such questions as what activities, possessions, and actions make you happy, fill you with delight, make you feel energized and optimistic, and what actions make you feel as if you count in your own eyes. These will lead you to your purpose.

Eric Maisel, in *Fearless Creating* (1995), asks if you don't already possess an idea that you've wanted to work on for a very long time that resurfaces unbidden, that you keep putting off, that you love but also doubt. You reject it because you can't see the whole picture, don't see it as commercially viable, fear it will require too much research, believe you just aren't equal to it, or you're sure someone else could do a better job with it or has already done a better job with it.

None of these are good reasons, says Maisel. Even if you don't know whether or not this idea is worth bringing back, Maisel suggests that you honor it, think about it, and cherish it. It is an idea that has been an integral part of you and at the very least deserves attention. It is also an idea that in high probability is connected to your purpose.

In *How to Live the Life You Love* (1996), Barbara Sher asks you to take your dreams one at a time and imagine having focused entirely on that one activity all your life, turning it into a profession, and going to the top of that profession. Then write down what your life is like and what you've done with this passion. Next take each fantasy out five years, still successful. "Now, how are you spending your time? Are you still doing the same things? Has it transmuted into something else?" You might even want to see what happens if you take this fantasy out yet another five years. It's often in these "post-success stories," life after success, life after achievement, when the most important activities show up in this exercise.

You don't have to make a living at fulfilling your purpose in the beginning, but you probably will one day, as long as you continue on that path. Although something you love may not be practical for you, there are always elements you love, perhaps themes, in these activities or fantasies that can be found in activities that you can do right now.

Some final words of wisdom from Sher, when you start doing what you love: "You will be moving and you will have a direction. Sometimes you're going to have to get there before you even realize that you've been going in the right direction all along."

# Chapter 38
# Managing States

> "To master ourselves is to arrive home at the center of being. . . What we seek, we already *are*."
> – *Lama Surya Das*

If you were in a nervous or shy state and wanted to be in a confident state, if you were in an angry state and wanted to be in a powerfully calm state, if you were in a confused state and wanted to be in a state of clarity, it would be useful – especially in connection with charisma – to be able to shift to the preferred state deliberately and quickly. Charismatic people appear to always be in control, particularly of themselves.

To manage your states means that you can decide at any moment how you wish to feel and behave. This does not mean that you will be faking the new state or being insincere. It also doesn't mean that you won't find yourself in negative states from time to time. Charismatic people have a way of, consciously or unconsciously, being able to shift to whatever state is the most empowering for any given circumstance. You will learn how to do this in a way that is congruent, honest, and best serves yourself and others.

Managing your states, however, is different than controlling your life. In an episode of the television series *The West Wing*, called "Celestial Navigation," the character Josh Lyman is being interviewed about a "typical day" working at the White House. He replies that there is no such thing: "It starts out as a 9-5 job, with a certain structure and schedule, but that's pretty much shot to hell by 9:30." That's the way life is. You can set up a structure and a plan, a schedule, but you can count on getting off course very quickly. A common example I've heard many speakers use is that a plane going from Los Angeles to Hawaii will be off course 95 percent of the time. The pilot doesn't panic because he or she is off course; the pilot just constantly makes corrections in order to land at the precise spot where he or she wants to land.

You cannot control many circumstances, but you *can* control how you interpret and react to a situation. This is how you can change states and still be true to your feelings. You can reinterpret what the event *means* to you (Chapter 15), and thus change the way you feel. You can also change what you're doing physiologically (Chapter 6), what you're focusing on (Chapter 18), how you're focusing (Chapter 20), and what words you use, both spoken and internal (Chapters 21 and 22).

Because charismatic people are in the present moment and are aware of what they are feeling, they have the option of changing their states to be appropriate to the situation in which they currently find themselves. This is obvious in charismatic people whose careers are in the arena of communication, such as actors, singers, dancers, politicians, and speakers. Their livelihood is in expressing a predetermined series of states. It doesn't matter how they "feel" or what circumstances they are going through personally. When they step on that stage or up to the podium or in front of the camera, they have to be able to call up a given state in a moment's notice, and be able to actually change how they feel. Martial artists, athletes, spiritual leaders, and others who exhibit charisma also have certain states they need to access, at a conscious or unconscious level, to "perform" at their peak. Additionally, they need to be able to shift out of any state that would distract them from the focus they need to have.

I've come up with a system for managing states, which I call "The Four Questions." The first question is, "How do I feel at the moment?" Don't spend a lot of time on this one. Especially if you are not feeling empowered, a brief description is all you need, just to have a starting point. It starts with being in the moment and in touch with your feelings.

The second question is, "How do I *want* to feel right now?" You might want to spend a little more time (at least to begin with) dwelling on this question to sharpen your focus on exactly how you do want to feel. If the answer to the first question found that you were already in a good state, ask yourself how it could be even better. Make a list of states that are empowering for you, so that you can practice shifting into them easily.

The third question is, "How would I feel if I felt the way I want to feel right now?" Practice each state and internalize it. Remember a time when you felt that way in the past and re-experience it, internally. If you've never felt that way before, imagine how you would feel if you *did* feel that way. You have to have an idea of how it would feel, otherwise how would you know that was how you wanted to feel and how would you know if you felt that way? Practice what you've previously learned, using your physiology, focus, internal representations, language, and self-talk. Now take that state to the next level. Make it brighter, bigger, and closer. If there is sound involved, turn up the volume or modify it however you need to in order to make it more powerful.

The fourth question you ask yourself is, "What's keeping me from feeling this way all the time or any time I want?" The answer is likely to be habit. It isn't something that very many people consider or consider often. Your thoughts and feelings are usually the thoughts and feelings you habitually have day in and day out. They could also be states that are habitually and unconsciously triggered by certain circumstances in your life.

Another answer might be because until now, you didn't make decisions about how you wanted to feel. You just felt the way you did without taking any initiative to change it. I recommend starting every morning with these questions. Then, take some deep breaths and proceed with your day deliberately, calmly, and with purpose.

Katharine Hepburn once referred to her arrival in Hollywood by saying, "I was bringing myself as though I were a basket of flowers!" She was carrying herself as if she were a beautiful gift. In that way, she also talked, walked, and moved as if she were already successful. And, there's certainly no doubt about *her* charisma!! She embodied the charismatic qualities of dignity, confidence, self-esteem, fearlessness, determination, and perseverance in her self-image.

# Chapter 39
# Nothing More Than Feelings

"All the emotions that you could ever have are nothing but physiological storms in your brain. Put your body in the right place, focus on things the right way, you feel them now."
– *Tony Robbins*

Medical doctor Deepak Chopra gets more specific in *Quantum Healing* (1989), describing how it is known scientifically, through PET (positron-emission tomography) scans, that thoughts and feelings interact with our physical bodies. Injected glucose reaches the brain, which is pictured on a monitor in three dimensions. The marker molecules of injected dye shift around while the brain thinks, allowing scientists to see that each distinct event in the mind – such as sensations, strong memories, and emotions – triggers a new chemical pattern in the brain. This happens at several sites simultaneously, not just at a single site. Chopra declares, "The image looks different for every thought, and if one could extend the portrait to be full-length, there is no doubt that the whole body changes at the same time, thanks to the cascades of neuro-transmitters and related messenger molecules."

Chopra continues to explain that your body is the physical picture, in 3-D, of what you are thinking. Since many physiological changes involve minute alterations of cell chemistry, body temperature, electrical charge, and blood pressure, which are not noticed on the outside, you don't usually see your body as projected thoughts. Chopra assures us, however, that "the body is fluid enough to mirror any mental event. Nothing can move without moving the whole…Mind is projected everywhere in inner space." Therefore, when you manage your states, you are also effecting physiological, mental, and emotional changes.

In *The Power to Shape Your Destiny* (2001), Tony Robbins indicates that when you think you are *feeling* stress, you are actually *doing* stress. You can reframe your perception of what most people consider a passive experience (feeling) into an active experience (doing). You become empowered when you realize that you create stress (or any state) by your thoughts and reactions; you are helpless, though, if you think you are a victim of stress. Robbins reminds us that, in order to be stressed, you have to use your body in a certain way, talk to yourself a certain way, and focus a certain way. He summarizes, "So, if you can do stress, you can choose, the minute you're aware of it, to do something else, called relaxation, or called courage, or called determination." When you have a certain feeling, consider that there might be a correlation between your posture, focus, and self-talk and the emotion. How might you change what you are doing in order to change how you are feeling? Experiment to feel how making adjustments changes the way you feel.

If you think your feelings are triggered by people and events outside of yourself, remember that the only meaning anything has is the meaning you give to it. It is your interpretation of the event or of what the person said or did that caused you to feel and react the way you did. Serge King, in *Positive Programming* (1988), tells us that our feelings are lousy guides to behavior or decisions. "When you get a negative feeling, it doesn't mean anything except that you've been thinking a negative thought or you've been performing some negative behavior." Feelings are energy flows. When you act because of your feelings, then you reinforce them, and you reinforce your thinking.

Method acting actually teaches how to control your states and project your feelings, putting you in the emotional state of your character by remembering a time you felt that way or imagining a situation in which you would feel the way your character would feel. To be effective, actors have to feel the emotion on the inside, not just pretend. Many actors are shy or insecure in their private lives, yet have a commanding and charismatic presence when working, because they manage their states when they act or are in public. They think of it as a skill of the trade, but they might accurately think of it as a life skill. I once read a book on acting technique that instructed to project the emotion through your eyes. This statement resonated with me. I would go further to say that first you feel the emotion throughout your entire body and then express it out through your eyes.

When practicing feeling and projecting various states, here are some that are conducive to charisma: passion, enthusiasm, joy, motivation, sense of purpose, confidence, peace, and love or being loved. Motivational speaker Wayne Dyer advises to "shift your sights to living and acting in rapport with your passion." This equates with Ralph Waldo Emerson, who stated, "Nothing great was ever achieved without enthusiasm." Enthusiasm and passion are wonderful states to be able to access. They are states that charismatic people are intimately familiar with.

Nijole Sparkis discussed that when you are in the moment and doing what you were born to do, you express love, which is charismatic. "The more we love what we do, the more we love the opportunity to do that which we love, the more we love ourselves by giving ourselves more opportunities to do that which we love, the more charismatic we become."

You can find some other powerful states by asking yourself why you want a certain goal or desire you have. When you discover what a goal or desire will give you, you will find that ultimately, it all comes down to how it will make you feel. Whatever that feeling is (pride, excitement, love, accomplishment, freedom, abundance – all of those are feelings), you can have all those feelings now. In *The Power to Shape Your Destiny* (2001), Tony Robbins reveals, "You have a bunch of rules – a bunch of beliefs – about what has to happen before you allow yourself to feel good...you unconsciously know how to create every emotion,' cause you create every emotion." You can still reach for any goal you desire, but just know that you can have the feeling it will give you before you reach the goal, then go for it! Why wait? Often, it actually increases your motivation, confidence, and self-esteem to experience how the end result would feel.

# Chapter 40
# Submodalities and Swishing

> "The swish pattern has a more powerful effect than any other technique I've used...It's a very generative pattern that programs your brain to go in a new direction."
> – *Richard Bandler*

Richard Bandler, the co-creator of NLP (Neuro-Linguistic Programming, a system of processes for successful strategies in self-development), introduced a process called "the swish pattern" that quickly becomes automatic for replacing unpleasant memories and undesired states with productive memories and states. This chapter picks up where Chapter 20 left off (you may want to review Chapter 20 before continuing) on internal representations, modalities, and submodalities, using them in a more advanced way.

In *Rare Bandler* (1982), Bandler discusses taking the internal representations you have of memories (the internal images, sounds, feelings, and even smells and tastes, when appropriate), and altering the submodalities, to change how you feel about your experiences. A basic exercise from Bandler's repertoire is to take an image of a mildly negative memory (nothing traumatic) and a second image, this one of a positive memory. With closed eyes, focus in on the internal images, sounds, and feelings of each memory. Play with the brightness and darkness of each image to see how it affects the intensity. Usually the brighter the image, the more intense the feeling, though in some people and in certain circumstances, it's the opposite.

Next, make the negative image large and bright, in the center of your imagination. Place the positive image in the lower left corner, small and dark. Now, enlarge the positive picture and make it very bright and large enough that it covers up the negative picture. Do this as slowly as you need to the first time, so you understand the process. Then, do it three times very quickly. Going back to the first picture, notice how you feel. *Try* to feel bad using the first image. The negative feeling will either be gone or, at least, different. If not, repeating the process at a faster speed will get you this result. Bandler teases his audience, "Why? Wasn't it a 'real' memory? If you can't feel bad in the same way, that's called change. And to me, that's a change that counts."

Through rapid repetition, the swish pattern sets up a sequence of associations and the negative image becomes connected to the positive image. As the negative is consistently followed with the positive, you're telling the mind *not* "this," but "*that.*" You take the mind from where it is to where you want it to be, and then leave it there.

Some additional tips on swish patterns from Richard Bandler come from *Personal Outcomes: Changing Responses* (1989). The results depend on the intensity of the second image. "That second picture that you build can't be ho-hum or the results won't last." You have to light up when you look at that picture. It's the most powerful when the image motivates you and you are drawn toward it. Find a time in the past when you felt a little assertive and turn up the brightness. Turn up the brightness on any images or experiences you have of yourself feeling charismatic. Making the image closer and panoramic usually intensifies the state as well. By going through and varying different submodalities, you can get some experiences to be more intense and more powerful than when they actually happened.

Bandler notes that people can get really angry by finding a time when they were a little angry and turning up the brightness. If you want to stop feeling angry, Bandler suggests putting a pleasant image in the corner and doing a swish pattern, bringing the pleasant image up to replace the old image. Another way to work with submodalities to get out of anger is described by Bandler in *Personal Outcomes: Motivation* (1989). In this seminar, there was an attendee who had difficulty controlling his anger. Through a series of questions, Bandler elicited that when this man was angry, he had a loud internal dialogue, very large pictures (blown out of proportion), with the images being very close and panoramic, and he was associated inside the picture. Bandler's solution: push the pictures off into the distance, make them smaller and farther away, and also push back the location of the internal dialogue and turn down the volume. The man tested these internal changes and instantly felt calm and in control.

Another example of submodality work is offered in Richard Bandler's *Personal Outcomes: Resolving Problems* (1989). Bandler has his attendees take two past memories – one of a situation that is over but still interfering with their lives; the other of a previous situation that doesn't matter anymore, but that used to be important – one that has changed in their minds (such as when they were kids and getting a bicycle was the most important thing in the world, and now that's something they don't care about at all). Then, he had them go through and find three or four submodalities that were different between the two images, such as location in the mind, size, distance, brightness, movie or slide, panoramic or borders, associated or dissociated, color or black and white, three-dimensional or two-dimensional. Next, he had them change the submodalities of the interfering "important" memory to the submodalities they found in the memory that is no longer important. For instance, if the memory that seems important is in color, directly in front of them, a movie, and they are associated in the memory, while the memory that is no longer important is to the lower left side, a slide in black and white, and they see themselves in the picture, they were to take the interfering memory and change the qualities to imagine it to the lower left, a black and white slide, and see themselves in the picture. This technique can also be used to discover how you motivate yourself and create motivation.

In the previous chapter I mentioned that passion is a powerful state to connect with. An attendee at a seminar of Bandler's mentioned that she had difficulty bringing up passion. Bandler suggested adding smells, tastes, and sounds. Passion is kinesthetic, and you can't get there with only visual submodalities. Charisma is also a kinesthetic state. A confident, powerful mental soundtrack can be helpful in creating charisma.

# Chapter 41
# Projecting Energy

"When you become aware of the amount of energy within you, you can focus it in a particular direction, with specific intention, and you give it specific qualities."
— *Tad James and David Shepherd*

When interacting with others, what you do mentally is just as important as your body language and what you say. Other people pick up on your emotional state and thoughts on an unconscious level. When you walk around worrying about your problems or focused on other negativities, that shows up in your aura and energy; others will be uncomfortable around you without consciously knowing why. One reason your mood or state changes when you are around others is because you are interacting with *their* energy and are unconsciously picking up their thoughts and emotions.

Christiane Northrup, in her PBS special, *Menopause and Beyond: New Wisdom for Women* (2007), offers the following technique. When you go out into public, imagine a large mirror over your head, reflecting the thoughts about yourself that you want projected to the world. If you think about it, this works with submodalities. You amplify inner images and voices, and you also make conscious decisions about which thoughts to focus on and project. As well as influencing the emotional state of others, this will also affect your own emotional state and create a feeling of inner strength and power.

Cesar Millan, "The Dog Whisperer," explains that animals know us by our energy, not by what we say. If you feel sorry for an animal or are fearful, anxious, nervous, frustrated, angry, or insecure, you are projecting a weak energy in the animal world and the animal will exhibit unstable or dominant behavior, as it will sense that you don't know how to lead. According to Millan, if you don't demonstrate to a dog that you are in control (a calm, assertive pack leader), the dog will reflect your insecure or unbalanced energy. They respond in a balanced way to calm, assertive energy. People do too. If you project an energy that you know what you're doing, people will tend to trust and believe you.

The charismatic Millan also says that he never begins an exercise with a dog without first deciding what he wants to accomplish and visualizing how he wants the exercise to go. He then makes sure his energy is calm and assertive and he "makes it happen." Once he has a clear image of his goal, he doesn't stop until he finds a way to fulfill it. He declares, "It's all about intention."

Lindy Baker, at a workshop (*Super Intuition*) during the 2007 American Board of Hypnotherapy convention, described her technique of "packing" qualities into your aura. Building on the concept that thought is real matter, she further explained that emotion "sticks" the thoughts into the atoms and the molecules around you.

The first step of her process is to write down what you want others to perceive about you as a first impression. How do you want people to feel about you? Make a list of associated words, symbols, and emotions that match the element you want to relay. Actually *feel* the words, symbols, and emotions, as that's what gives them life to project the energy. The vibrational rate of joy is good for building and projecting energy. Try combining this emotion with the words, symbols, and emotions you want to project.

The last step in Baker's method, after working up the emotion, is to take four or five of these elements and "slam" them into your aura. Imagine taking each one in your hands and, physically using your hands, slam them all around your body into your aura. Then imagine "saving" them there.

Tad James and David Shephard (*Presenting Magically*, 2001) also claim that you can put desirable qualities into the energy you send out. Similar to what Baker teaches, think about the qualities you would like to have in the space around you and imagine putting those qualities into the energy you are sending out. "With every breath out, push that energy into the room. You may find this easier if you give the energy a colour and a sound." Here we are back to using modalities and submodalities. Envision pushing the energy out so that everybody who comes into touch with that energy feels what you are projecting. You may even want to use your hands to assist you in pushing the energy out.

Although the James/Shepherd book is designed for people presenting workshops or lectures, many of the techniques can apply in a number of situations, including performances and business meetings. An extension of the previous exercise to use for interacting with a group of people is to imagine your energy in your mind's eye, pushing the energy out so that it encompasses everybody. Be sure to include yourself, extending the energy around and behind you. When you are using peripheral vision to put a ring of energy around everyone in the group, your attention is on everyone, and your energy is flowing to everyone at the same time. When you pull that energy ring in a little, tightening it slightly, the energy in the room will intensify.

Remember the Roger Dawson quote at the beginning of Chapter 26: "Charisma is a matter of expanding your sense of self to embrace all the people with whom you come in contact." James and Shepherd put it this way: "Even before you start, stand where you are going to be presenting on the stage, and fill all the space with your energy, of the appropriate quality.

Expand your energy field to fill the entire space, so that it is part of you."

Your state is projected in your energy. When projecting the energy you've decided on, make sure that your state reinforces that energy.

# Chapter 42
# Nuances of Charisma

> "There are definitely times when I feel less charisma or "magic" on stage than other times...I usually blame it on quality of sleep, food, or just plain old mood. But charisma is different than just a good show."
>
> – *Kyle Vincent*

This is kind of a "catchall" chapter, where I'm putting thoughts and observations that either are variables or don't fit in any other chapter.

As charisma is a state, there are varying degrees of it; it is not a case of, as the saying goes, "Either you have it or you don't." Even when you consider someone to be charismatic, he or she typically does not have the same degree of charisma at all times. Many performers who are charismatic onstage or on screen are not charismatic in their personal lives. This also goes along with being a state, in that it can depend on the situation, who you're around, and other considerations. Your belief system plays an important role too. There are highly evolved spiritual leaders who are extremely charismatic all the time, and they meet all of the criteria I put forth in my study. They are rare, but they do exist.

Charisma can be either natural or learned. I believe it is a part of our spirit that we are all born with, and that if we don't exhibit it, it's because it has remained dormant or we have "unlearned" it when growing up. Inherent qualities can be unlearned because of the way we were treated, what we were told by family or the education system, or other influences (including modeling people close to us, as we do in our formative years). If we don't use a part of ourselves, it's still there, but is no longer apparent. Kyle Vincent is a typical case in that his charisma is naturally occurring and also variable: "I do feel a certain special light or electricity when I'm on stage, but I also feel 'it' shopping at the farmer's market or when I'm planting a tree. It's always there."

Charisma can be like singing; some people have powerful or beautifully effortless voices naturally, and others with great voices have studied diligently, learning the various elements of music separately, working to combine them in just the right way. With practice, it becomes second nature so they don't have to think about it anymore. Many of the problems people have with voice control result from poor habits they have gotten into, and not because there is anything inherently wrong with their voices or that they have "bad" voices. A lot of the work to be done is actually "undoing" inadvertent habits.

Charisma is also subjective in that each observer will perceive a specific individual's charisma differently, being filtered through their own experiences, beliefs, and values.

It can be difficult to reconcile that there are also decidedly *un*spiritual people, like Hitler and cult leaders, who have been considered to be charismatic. This has to do with their belief systems, sense of personal power, self-confidence, and sense of purpose. Being primarily delusional, these distorted personalities can be charismatic while being congruent with their own beliefs and values. Their followers, mostly people who are in an insecure or vulnerable state and looking for guidance, must also hold certain beliefs and values that allow them to unfortunately be attracted to this kind of energy.

I want to acknowledge an "artificial charisma" that exists, which appears to be charisma, but isn't really charisma at all. It's built on press, hype, spin, and public appearances. It doesn't come from the person directly (like authentic charisma does), but basically from marketing (primarily political figures, but some celebrities too). Of course, there are many politicians and celebrities who project genuine charisma. Other people can perceive the artificial variety as charisma unless they know or have contact with the person directly, where the facade is revealed. This isn't the type of charisma that this book is about, but it warrants mentioning, since many people wonder about it.

Additionally, there are individuals who are in between hype and charisma (a little of both) by design, and there are also those who have or have developed a natural, effortless charisma at times, but who also need to use some intention at other times.

Something that Kyle Vincent brought up in my interview with him raises another issue. He felt he didn't get the attention he needed or wanted as a child and speculated that there could be a connection between charisma and seeking validation. I found that very interesting, as it seems to be a common theme with many charismatic personalities. I refer to it as the Marilyn Monroe complex. Her childhood was very lonely and she developed many insecurities. Many performers go into the entertainment field to get desired attention. The mass adoration they attain creates the state of feeling loved, which they don't feel otherwise. But that is just an interpretation; they have decided this means they are loved, and then they feel loved.

You know by now that at any time you choose, you can create any feeling you want to create. You also have the power to decide what any given situation means.

✧ ✧ ✧

# Chapter 43
# Confidence

> "True confidence...comes from a commitment you make to yourself, a commitment that you will do whatever it is that you want and need to do in life."
> – *Barbara DeAngelis*

Confidence is a state. It's something you *feel*. You can look at someone you've never seen before or someone you know nothing about and get a sense that person is confident. If someone lacks confidence, it will typically be reflected in the person's body language and speech. Because it's a state, you can be confident in some situations and not in others.

I see confidence as a component state of charisma. Although confident people are not necessarily charismatic, I believe that when people are in a charismatic state, they are always confident. You don't need to be extroverted to show confidence. Those who are charismatically confident can be calm or impassioned, but they always have a sense of being centered or balanced, in the present moment, and able to manage their states. This does not mean that they are always happy or enthusiastic. When they are upset or angry, for example, they find a way to channel the emotion productively, to their benefit, or convert it to a more advantageous state, such as being assertive, but calm and coherent.

Confidence is not based on your level of ability in what you are doing, or even how you feel about your current abilities. Barbara DeAngelis, in *Confidence: Finding It and Living It* (1995), explains, "It is founded on a trust in you, not a trust in the outcomes you may or may not achieve." DeAngelis later elaborates, "Confidence is born of your belief in your own integrity, your commitment that

171

whatever you want, you're going to work hard to achieve it." You may not know *how* to achieve it, or even feel certain that you *will* achieve it, but having confidence means you know and trust that you will do whatever it takes, one step at a time.

You can increase your feeling of confidence very quickly, simply by accomplishing something that brings you one step closer to one of your goals. Your confidence will instantly grow, because you'll trust that you can count on yourself. The more steps you take, the better you'll feel about yourself, and that new confidence will help you create better results. However, you'll develop a truer sense of confidence when you push yourself further than your current abilities, expanding your comfort zone.

Although people who are confident appear to be fearless, this can be deceptive. Confident people still have fears, but will act in spite of those fears, giving a fearless appearance. They understand that fears and doubts are powerless if you treat them as being unimportant. When you fight, deny, or suppress your fears, you give them power, implying that they are important. If they were not important, you wouldn't feel the need to do anything about them. Of course, you want to honor any fear or doubt that might result in bodily harm, but if the fear or doubt is nothing more than a mental or emotional obstacle to accomplishing a goal; if you are confident, you can brush it aside. If this fear or doubt is based on a specific past experience, it would be wise to ascertain if you might learn from the past experience something that would reduce current or future risks, before you proceed. This in itself could reduce the feeling of fear or doubt.

You may make many mistakes or come up against several obstacles, but if you don't give up, knowing you won't give up, you will continue to have the confidence of a charismatic individual. If you stop pursuing a dream, you break that confidence. You lose trust in yourself. When you have confidence, you will not be concerned about whether or not you look perfect or avoid mistakes. You will be willing to not look good and go forward anyway.

Being a state, there is a physiology to confidence, just as there is a physiology to charisma. You know how someone who is confident would stand or sit, how that person would breathe, talk, and gesture. When you begin to take on the posture and body language of confidence, there is an internal shift, and you begin to think and act differently. When you see someone else in a powerful state (confident, charismatic, enthusiastic), you will often unconsciously adjust your own posture to be in rapport with him or her. A powerful state, especially when produced with intention, can be very contagious. This is part of the effectiveness of successful motivational speakers. They direct or lead you to mirror their own passionate state. The problem arises, though, when you don't realize how your motivated state is achieved. After you leave a motivational speech, you may not be able to recapture the desired state that was achieved during the presentation, and then give up, thinking you were just carried away during the talk and don't really have what it takes to accomplish your dreams after all.

You can also affect your confidence by your language, both in what you say to yourself and in what you say to other people. People who are confident use a different vocabulary than people who lack confidence. Changing your physiology, which changes your emotions, changes the way you think and the way you talk to yourself. Changing the way you talk to yourself also changes your emotions and your physiology.

Another way you can manage your state is by utilizing your imagination. Richard Bandler (*Personal Outcomes: Motivation,* 1989) worked with a woman in a seminar who was uncomfortable around people. He asked her if there was ever a time when she *was* comfortable around people. When she said there was, but didn't understand why, he asserted, "At those times you forget to do the things that make you feel uncomfortable – the pictures you show yourself or the internal dialog you start up."

Since she was having difficulty with this concept, Bandler came up with a clever way for her to discover her own strategy. He expressed the idea that she should be able to take a day off from her personal problems, to go on vacation from them, and have a day when she could go out and just feel comfortable around people. The way he proposed this was for her to hire *him* to have this problem *for* her for a day. All she had to do was to give him a job description.

With some prodding, she saw that she began the behavior before she was even in the situation. She began the disempowering self-talk and images on the way to the event or gathering. This process dissociated her from the experience, looking at analyzing what she did (rather than experiencing the feelings) and also transferring thinking of it as *her* behavior to imagining how *someone else* would have the behavior. Bandler also implied that she could leave the behavior behind.

Bandler expressed the belief that this strategy requires adequate planning. "If you really want to be disappointed, you've got to make a real big plan to have it not come off." He then used a metaphor, describing his experience of dating. He had to make specific images about the date, and if it didn't happen that way, he'd be disappointed. "I found, if I don't make those kinds of images ahead of time, then I just have fun. Kind of ruins the whole thing! I have nothing to complain about at the end of the night!"

✯ ✯ ✯

# Chapter 44
# Decisiveness

> "Each decision we make, whether large or small, defines who we are and the quality of person we are becoming."
> – *Valerie Wells*

Charismatic people are decisive. When you are decisive, you claim your power by making conscious decisions based on your strengths and positive motivations. Every day you are faced with dozens of choices, both major and minor. You make some decisions thoughtfully on a conscious level, some automatically on an unconscious level, and just ignore making other decisions. Obviously, you can't make every decision consciously; you wouldn't have time to do anything else. Most decisions are so minor, inconsequential, or repetitive, that there is no reason to give them any further consideration than you currently do.

However, you might want to occasionally spend some time focusing your awareness on your decision-making process, to see if you might be habitually making some decisions out of fear or another motivation based on your perceived weaknesses.

In *Power Living by Jake* (1997), Jake Steinfeld cautions that some people don't achieve success because they don't understand the difference between making a decision and making a wish. "When you make a decision, you commit to taking an action that propels you forward. You leave all other options behind. When you make a wish, you are not committing to taking an action, so you remain stationary. A wish changes nothing. A decision changes *everything*." Charismatic people make decisions, not wishes.

Tony Robbins goes even further in *The Power to Shape Your Destiny* (2001) by declaring, "It's in your moments of decision that your destiny is shaped." Robbins elaborates in *Personal Power!* (1993), reasoning that every thought you think or action you take is a cause set in motion, which then has a result or impact in your life. These results add up, taking you in a particular direction for which there is an ultimate destination or destiny. Therefore, your every thought, decision, or action, cumulatively affects your destiny. It makes sense, then, to make decisions with greater purpose.

Many successful people start one career and find success in a completely different area. However, they were doing *something* when the right opportunity came along. They were taking some action, leading them to what they were supposed to be doing. History shows us that circumstances often don't turn out as planned, and charismatic people are flexible, making decisions and taking actions without being attached to the outcomes.

Roger Dawson (*Secrets of Power Persuasion*, 1992) emphasizes, "Sometimes it's less important that you make the right decision than that you make a decision, any decision. There's a tremendous release of energy that comes from the decision to move in a particular direction." Your energy level drops the longer you take to decide. Once a direction is picked, you immediately feel better and can concentrate more clearly.

Barbara Sher (*How to Live the Life You Love,* 1996) believes that planning is nothing but science fiction because you can't see into the future. "But, plans are great anyway. So, if you can pick a goal and plan it and go after it, very random amazing things will happen to you, none of which you planned. But that's the best reason to do it."

Cherie Carter-Scott (*If Success Is a Game, These Are the Rules,* 2000) asserts that you won't know in advance which choices are the right ones and which are the wrong ones. "You just make the choice that feels right to you at that time, and you follow that route either toward success or toward the lessons you were meant to learn."

# Chapter 44: Decisiveness

At some point, you may decide to revise your map or change your destination entirely. This doesn't mean that you made the wrong choice or that you failed. Instead, it means that you wisely altered your original plan once you had more data. Charismatic people are flexible to changing circumstances or perspectives.

There are many strategies for making decisions we consider to be difficult. One of my favorite is the coin toss approach, which comes from a poem I once read as a child. I don't remember the exact words, but the gist of it is that in order to make a decision that conflicts you internally, toss a coin up in the air – not so the coin will tell you which way to decide, but because when the coin is up in the air, you'll suddenly know which answer you were hoping for (or which one is best). This demonstrates that you always know the answer within you, but you don't always trust that you know.

When making complex decisions that will have a major impact in your life or the lives of others, you might be likely to take a more disciplined approach, checking in with your head, your heart, and your gut, instead of following just one.

When checking in with your head, make a list of options, pros and cons, and every aspect you think might be relevant to making this decision, clarifying your priorities. The purpose of getting thoughts out of your head and on to paper, where they can be addressed one by one, is that when thoughts are trapped inside your mind they can look distorted and more complicated or convoluted than they may really be.

To explore your emotions, imagine yourself in the new situation; tune in, and notice the feelings the image evokes. Observe if you feel energized, depleted, overwhelmed, excited, silly, or powerful. Pay attention to your physical reactions. Clues to how you really feel might be in changes in your breathing, stress slowly creeping into your shoulders, butterflies in your stomach, or a throbbing sensation in your temples. You might feel lighter, almost lofty, or you might feel overwhelming responsibility or burden. Write all these feeling observations down on paper. This

new behavior generator

act will help discharge the emotions from your psyche, so your ability to make a clear choice is enhanced.

At this point, you can set aside your mental and emotional processes and listen for your internal gut response, or intuition. Carter-Scott tells us, "You can access your gut only when you are calm, quiet, and centered within yourself…Neither emotions nor logic temper it. It is clear, certain, and absolute…similar to those moments when you realize in hindsight that your initial intuition was accurate."

You might think you "don't know," because you don't think what you really want is possible. Asking yourself some questions in a light state of trance can bring a creative solution. You might ask, "What would it take to make all this work?" or "What would the ideal look like?" or "If I *did* know what I wanted here, what would it be?"

Michael Yapko (*Trancework*, 1990) describes how Milton Erickson had his patients, in trance, project themselves into the future, using one behavior or course of action, and have them report on where that led them. He would then give them a different behavior or course of action and ask them to describe to him where they wound up if they made that decision. Another exercise he would have them do was to produce a desirable outcome in the future and have them look back to see how it was accomplished.

✦ ✦ ✦

# Chapter 45
# Choice

> "You choose only what you believe is possible to choose, and these choices determine what you do with your life and who you become."
> – *Grandmaster Tai Yun Kim*

What you do, how you live, and what you become, is almost entirely up to you. Of course there are outside circumstances to deal with, but how you deal with them is still, and finally, up to you. What you decide to do next will determine what you do next. If you let the world decide for you, it will, and the result is usually not what you would have chosen for yourself, if you had accepted your power and been decisive.

Whenever you are faced with two or more options, you can choose from three available strategies. All three of these strategies can be executed with awareness or automatically, without awareness. The more awareness you have, the greater your choices will be. The strategies are:

1) <u>Give your power away</u>

You can choose to give your power away by letting someone else or circumstances make the decision for you. I am not referring here to a situation such as going out with friends or loved ones and letting someone else pick the movie or restaurant, in the spirit of taking turns, but when you intentionally avoid making decisions for yourself. Although someone or something else is making the specific decision, it is your decision (or choice) to allow it. The behavior may be conscious or unconscious, based on fear, insecurity, manipulation, or other motivation when you believe you lack power. You may also want to avoid responsibility, but you are giving away your power only, as you are still responsible for giving the decision to someone else or circumstances to make.

You can also decide not to make any changes in your life, even though you know it would be in your best interest to do so. You are then stuck in your current situation. In *Dick Clark's Program for Success* (1980), Dick Clark explains why it's so difficult to get moving in a new direction. "Years of stagnation give a person the feeling that forward movement is impossible. Then, when a little bit of momentum is finally achieved, the person gets frightened that 'things are going too fast.' After all, in comparison to a living death, any movement at all is experienced as unstable and uncontrollable." Therefore, you choose not to move at all. If there does happen to be movement, then it will not be of your choosing, as you have basically decided that you either don't have or don't want the power to influence your life.

## 2) Block your power

The second strategy is that you can block your power by being indecisive and agonizing over the decision, seemingly not knowing which way to go. You can fret and let the issue stew in your mind. This causes not only mental stress, but also physical tension, and drains your energy, paralyzing you. Unless you learn how to push through this frustration, you will likely do nothing. This is not the same thing as deciding not to make a decision at all, as discussed in the previous paragraph, or deciding not to make a decision at this time, which can sometimes be smart if you require more information or if the time is not yet right.

Sometimes you may argue against yourself, creating an inner conflict, when you don't think that what you really want to do is practical or achievable. You have a gut feeling, but you are afraid to follow it. Cherie Carter-Scott (*If Success Is a Game, These Are the Rules*, 2000) explains, "The reason that you didn't listen to your gut is either because it was unreasonable or it required you taking a risk. That is precisely what causes people to move into

'I don't know.'" "I don't know" is a safe response. It is the one that ensures you will not have to face your underlying fears.

Carter-Scott offers another reason for "I don't know." "You may not like the answer that surfaces…If you don't like the answer that arises, you might bury it without even realizing it and become caught in a false state of uncertainty." At some level within you, though, you usually do know the answer if you listen for it and trust yourself. There are exercises in the previous chapter for working through "I don't know."

3) <u>Claim your power</u>

Thirdly, you can claim your power and be decisive, confidently choosing for yourself, allowing input from others when appropriate. People who are decisive and charismatic understand Grandmaster Tai Yun Kim's teaching in *Seven Steps to Inner Power* (1991): "The truth is, you are exactly where you are because of the way you answered 'Who am I?' Why? Because how you answer the question determines the *choices* you make for yourself moment to moment every day of your life."

Valerie Wells (*Naturally Powerful*, 1999) declares, "The very act of making a decision is empowering. Even if it later becomes apparent that it was not the best decision, you have a better chance of succeeding if you set things in motion, rather than remaining static."

Charismatic people expect more from themselves than anyone else would ever ask of them. Some decisions are not linked to presenting options, but have to be sought out. They are decisions to take actions that will change your life and will come up only if you choose to bring them up yourself. If you are in a job you are comfortable in and have no reason to seek employment elsewhere, but you recognize a desire within yourself to pursue another line of work, you might take some classes, do some volunteer or part-time work in this area, or talk with people who are already doing this work. Only someone who claims his or her power will take those kinds of actions. Of course, this would also require confidence, a healthy self-esteem, and self-motivation. This is the mind-set of the charismatic person.

The creative process of decision-making for most people has been largely unconscious and therefore undirected, somewhat haphazard, and also influenced by other people's thinking and limited by their restricted awareness of what they think is possible. You can now realize that at any moment of conscious awareness you have the power to choose how to think, feel, or act.

It is human to want to avoid making mistakes, and that may be another reason you avoid being decisive. However, you can reframe what most people consider to be undesirable, as evidenced by Grandmaster Tai Yun Kim in *Seven Steps to Inner Power* (1991): "Here's the fact about mistakes. They are part of a natural feedback system in learning a task or accomplishing a goal. That's all." Kim goes on to say, "Mistakes are also essential to your progress. The minute you decide to achieve a goal that's important to you, you will make mistakes." The object is to succeed, not to count your mistakes. You can experience a new sense of freedom and increased energy when you no longer worry about defending or hiding your mistakes, but see them as friends and teachers. A whole world of choices will then open up to you.

✫ ✫ ✫

# Chapter 46
# Self-Motivation

> "The people who step up to the plate and actually swing the bat are the ones who are in the game and ultimately the ones who score. If you don't swing at the ball, how can you ever expect to hit a home run?"
> – *Cherie Carter-Scott*

It takes self-motivation to step up to the plate and to develop the skills necessary to play a winning game. You can be temporarily motivated by another person or a passing idea. However, if you don't understand what it is that motivates you or are not able to recreate that motivation in yourself when you get back to the details and distractions of everyday life, your old programming will quietly re-convince you that you are not capable of what you believed when you were listening to the speaker or daydreaming about your objectives.

Because charismatic people know how to manage their states, they can achieve a state of motivation at will. With this ability, you can call up the enthusiasm and passion to commit to a goal, project, or ideal and rev up your determination, so you will persevere until you get where you want to be. Charismatic people take action on the decisions they make, and they don't rely on anyone else to motivate them. In the same way that making a decision, any decision, releases energy and allows you to think more clearly, taking action, even one small step, creates momentum to take the next step, and the next.

Cherie Carter-Scott (*If Success Is a Game, These Are the Rules*, 2000) says to start with small steps. "Starting with small steps isn't because you aren't able to handle anything that is more challenging, but because it will help your self-confidence to see immediate results."

The fear of leaving the known for the unknown can block your motivation, since in order to move on, you have to leave some place or something behind. Although this can be exciting, it can also be scary. There is both the thrill of the anticipation and the uncertainty of what you may run into. That's why people with charisma either are naturally or have learned to be great risk-takers.

External motivations of "have to," "need to," "should," or "supposed to" cause stress, as it's only human to rebel against these concepts, which imply that you don't have a choice. According to Marsha Sinetar (*Do What You Love, The Money Will Follow*, 1987), "Such a nose-to-the-grindstone attitude is not even a good formula for success. When you study people who are successful. . . it is abundantly clear that their achievements are directly related to the enjoyment they derive from their work."

If you have difficulty finding motivation, Grandmaster Tai Yun Kim (*Seven Steps to Inner Power*, 1991), gives an example that may assist you. Imagine paying a tailor $1,000 in advance to produce evening clothes for wearing one time only at a special event. Kim asks if you would go to pick up your new clothes if it's raining, if you're angry over a late start because your stew boiled over, if you find your street blockaded by road construction, if the freeway traffic is totally stopped and you have to sit for two hours. "Of course" is the answer to all of these questions. And if you arrive at the tailor's just after he hung the "Closed" sign you'll bang on the door until he lets you in.

But when you're doing something for yourself, Kim inquires, "where does all this determination go…when, after more failures than you expected, you give in to fear and dejection? Are your new clothes really so much more deserving of your determination than *you* are?" When you need to motivate yourself, find or imagine considerable value in the investment you've made in yourself or your project.

When you have a purpose or aspire to an achievement, experience some joy or pride in achieving this goal. See some application to who you are or who you see yourself becoming. Find a compelling reason to motivate yourself and cause you to take action.

One way to generate motivation is to become a great student. When you strive to become an expert in your chosen field, without ever thinking that you know it all, motivation can become effortless, as motivation grows out of a curious and fascinated mind. An attitude of fascination can make any experience an interesting and beneficial learning opportunity. Wayne Dyer (*Inspiration: Your Ultimate Calling*, 2006) encourages, "Look for opportunities to verify your greatness, and expand your view of yourself..."

Asking the right questions can give you focus and help you to stay motivated and resourceful. If you are inquisitive and always asking yourself questions that excite you, you will become more motivated. That's why young children, who are always curious and asking questions, are naturally energetic and motivated.

You can use submodalities to facilitate internal shifts. When you imagine what it is you want to be motivated about, you can play with changing the submodalities of the internal representations you have (Chapters 20 and 40). Typically, turning still images into movies or making the movies faster, bringing the image closer and/or making it panoramic, making the images brighter or more colorful, adding sound and/or making the sound louder, faster, or changing the location of the sound are often ways of motivating yourself.

You might gain some insight if you listen to what you are telling yourself about your motivation or lack of motivation. I used to have difficulty getting out of bed in the morning. Then I noticed my habitual conversation with myself when I awoke. I would say,

"I don't want to get up," and "I just want to stay here and go back to sleep." I also used a slow, drowsy internal tone with these words. I broke this pattern by paying attention to what I was saying and how I was saying it, and changing the content to reflect the feelings and behavior I desired to have. I also sped up the internal dialog and gave it an exciting, energetic tone. If I have trouble going to sleep at night, often because of swirling thoughts, I reverse the process, dramatically slowing down my internal dialog, lowering the pitch, making it sound drowsy and saying, "I just can't stay awake another minute." It's not difficult to fool your mind. Think of other ways you can use this trick.

# Chapter 47
# Responsibility to Self

> "By being strong, [you] must be willing to take the consequences of that power and let go of the pretense, however unconsciously buried, that [you] are helpless. Perhaps it is easier to believe we have little potential than to admit our talents."
> – *Marsha Sinetar*

In the above quote, Marsha Sinetar (*Do What You Love, The Money Will Follow,* 1987) claims that most people have a secret prejudice against their own strengths, talents, and greatness, and turn away from growing and seeing their own potential. You have a responsibility to yourself, though, to uncover your talents and reach your goals.

Ben Sweetland (*I Can,* 1953) observed that when two or more people enter into any kind of a business arrangement of importance, a contract is usually drawn up. He asserts that we would be better off if we were to become obligated in some specific manner for the promises we make to ourselves.

Sweetland relates a story about one evening when he was getting ready to go to bed and thought about the day. Nothing of importance had happened. Then he remembered promises he had made to himself over the weekend on how he would start the week. He failed to follow through. "These, however, were merely promises but, as usual, the week had started and none of them were kept." He equates the way he felt that night to the straw that broke the camel's back. He was thoroughly disgusted with himself. Realizing how undependable he was, the thought crossed his mind that if a child continually disobeyed, he most likely would exert himself to find a remedy. Yet he had never done anything to try to correct his disobedience to himself. Then he got an idea. For one week he would keep every promise he made to himself, carefully weighing it beforehand to make sure he could keep the pledge. Because habit is so powerful, this was not easy to do at first. "I resolved to do certain things the following day, and when the next day arrived, was tempted to slide along and sidetrack the promise. But I stuck to my resolution. I actually forced myself to do the things I had laid out to do. By the end of the week I had made such strides – and felt so much more satisfied with myself – I determined to continue on the routine of self-discipline."

He emphasizes, however, that this does not mean spending every waking moment accomplishing something. It is equally important to arrange the day to accommodate rest and recreation. Sweetland also notes that while living according to this new routine of self-discipline, he thoroughly enjoyed his rest periods, as his mind would be at peace, and not confused with a myriad of promises he should have kept, but didn't.

When you continually and habitually make promises to yourself that you don't keep, you lose self-confidence. Do you make New Year's resolutions each year that you often don't keep or don't keep for very long? The reason you don't keep these promises is obvious. Usually, you are the only one who knows of these promises, and you figure that if no one else knows, it doesn't matter whether you actually do or don't do what you set out for yourself. You will not intentionally punish yourself for not doing something. However, you pay a very high price in lost confidence and self-respect, as you know on some level that you can't trust yourself to keep your own promises.

When you lack confidence, you may procrastinate, overanalyze your options, avoid challenging issues (or convince yourself they aren't really important, so you don't have to attend to them). You may not ask for help when you need it, you may be judgmental, either of yourself or others, or you may not trust yourself to make decisions.

In *Breaking the Chain of Low Self-Esteem* (1998), Marilyn Sorensen explains, "Submitting to the wishes of someone else frees us from the responsibility and the possibility of making a mistake…we can't make the wrong decision if we aren't making any decisions at all." When you let someone else make all the decisions for you, however, you also have no control. You only have control when you're making decisions for yourself. Therefore, when you lack confidence, you will also feed low self-esteem.

You may also be afraid that you would have to quit your "day job" and spend all your time on your purpose. However, you can take safe steps toward the larger goal of being your best self or discovering what you were meant to do by thinking of small, inconsequential ways to live out activities you enjoy in everyday life. Your purpose will grow naturally without taking drastic actions or changing everything at once.

In *Unlimited Energy* (1998), Peter McLaughlin quotes Stanford psychologist Albert Bandura, who reveals, "People's beliefs about their abilities have a profound effect on those abilities. Ability is not a fixed property – there is a huge variability in how you perform." In other words, if you doubt your abilities, you will not perform at your optimum level and, in fact, may never find out what the limits of your abilities are. This might cause a self-fulfilling prophecy, reinforcing your belief in your lack of talent.

You may doubt that you have the resources to fulfill the purpose you desire, but Richard N. Bolles (*The Three Boxes of Life*, 1981) believes that you have more control over your life than you think. He tells a story of a woman he worked with who was paralyzed with multiple sclerosis. Both a neurologist and a psychiatrist had examined her, and both said there was nothing they could do for her. She felt hopeless, as all her doctors told her she would just have to learn to live with it.

After determining that neither Bolles nor his client knew exactly what multiple sclerosis was, he suggested that they suppose that it was almost purely physical, caused by perhaps a virus that they had no control over, and for which the doctors had no cure. Supposing that 98 percent of it was physical, there would still be another 2 percent that *was* under the control of hidden forces within the patient – emotions or something that was consciously or unconsciously under the control of her will. Assuming that all they could work on was the 2 percent, or whatever the percentage was, she agreed to meet with him regularly so that they could work on that part of her disease that was within her control and power. Bolles summarizes, "In time, she lost so much of the paralysis, that she was able to resume a normal life. In fact, she became a clothes model, on fashionable 57th Street in New York. P. S. The doctors, of course, attributed this change to 'spontaneous remission, which is typical of this disease.' All I know is that Maryann worked very hard on that 'spontaneous remission.'"

No matter how much of your life you perceive to be unchangeable or in the control of someone or something else, there is always some part that is under your control. And it's almost always more than you think.

You might play victim to discharge yourself from any responsibility for your life. After all, clearly what is happening to you is not your fault. Even though you are often at the mercy of forces that you have no control over, there is a vast difference between being a victim (which we all are, in some areas of our life) and having a victim mentality. When you are a victim, you face powerful obstacles, but you confront them anyway and become stronger or more knowledgeable. Whereas, when you have a victim mentality, you give up, thinking that you don't have any power and that there is no use in continuing on that path. You have to give up a victim mentality to overcome fear and claim your responsibility to yourself.

# Chapter 48
# Self-Esteem

> "One's self-esteem is the subjective assessment of one's value as a human being. It is formed in part by the feedback one gets from others, but it is formed to a large extent by one's belief system."
> – *Michael Yapko*

The value you place on yourself is a learned rather than inborn phenomenon, based on your experiences and, more particularly, the conclusions you draw from those experiences, determining what you think you're capable of doing. Charismatic people believe that they can achieve any attainable goal to which they are committed.

You have a picture in your head that you believe represents who you are, by which you measure your worth, your competence, your worthiness, and your ability to cope and succeed in life. This may not be the perception that others have of you, but it dictates how you approach or avoid life, the ways you act and react, and your hopes for the future.

People with low self-esteem have images of themselves and inner voices formulated primarily or entirely on negative interpretations of past experiences, and thus label themselves as less worthy or less competent than others. In *Breaking the Chain of Low Self-Esteem* (1998), Marilyn Sorensen explains that people with low self-esteem, "seem to tightly grasp and even nurture the negative reruns so these memories actually grow in size and importance…the person focuses on his failures, weaknesses, unattained skills, and imperfections as though these were the only pieces of relevant, reliable information available." It's easy to see that this could never describe one who is charismatic.

The strongest force in the human personality is the need to remain consistent with how you define yourself. If you didn't remain consistent, you'd have an identity crisis. One mistake people make is to attach their identities to a past behavior or emotion. Tony Robbins (*The Power to Shape Your Destiny*, 2001) explains, "If you believe that's who you are, then you won't believe you can change. You are not your behavior; you are not your feelings. Both of those things change..." Consider when you came up with an unfavorable label for yourself and how much you and your life have changed since then.

Brian Tracy (*Action Strategies for Personal Achievement*, 1993) informs us, "You always perform on the outside consistent with the picture that you hold of yourself on the inside. . . it's possible for you to dramatically improve your performance by systematically changing the pictures that you hold about yourself in that area."

While it's true that many celebrities are known to suffer from self-esteem issues in their private lives, some that are quite severe, when they are in a charismatic state, they are accessing their self-empowering beliefs and connecting with their confidence and competence. Although you can't attain 100 percent positive, empowering beliefs, you *can* achieve predominantly empowering beliefs by being aware of what your beliefs are in the moment and applying techniques to make them more empowering. The more consistently you can feel good about yourself, the more charismatic you will be.

People with a healthy self-esteem do not want to defer their choices and decisions to others, as people with low self-esteem do. They value the freedom and accompanying responsibility that enables them to be in charge of their own lives, but they also allow others the freedom and responsibility to run *their* own lives as well.

They respect the beliefs, ideas, and feelings of others, as they do their own. They also don't hide their feelings out of fear of what other people might think or, conversely, push their ideas onto others, trying to dominate them.

You may recognize some hidden self-esteem issues when pondering Marilyn Sorensen's assuring "Things to Remember" (*Breaking the Chain of Low Self-Esteem*, 1998):

"Everyone makes mistakes. Making a mistake does not mean you are inadequate or incompetent.

"Everyone does things they later regret.

"Everyone has embarrassing moments.

"Others are not as aware of what you say or do as you are. They are usually focused on their own concerns.

"Being likable does not mean that everyone will like you.

"Everyone experiences rejection, whether in job interviews, possible romantic relationships, or simply by insensitive people.

"Everyone experiences disapproval. You can't please everyone all the time.

"Being imperfect is not synonymous with being inadequate. No one is perfect!"

In *Personal Outcomes: Motivation* (1989), Richard Bandler says that if you listen to what you say you want to change, you will actually explain how you could change it, using submodalities. One man came to him and said he wanted a "higher self-image."

Bandler asked him where his self-image currently was located in his imagination. It was directly in front of him between waist and chest height. Bandler asked him what it was attached to, and discovered it was on a vertical metal bar. Bandler then instructed him to move the image up to a comfortable spot, and stick a clamp on the bar underneath the image so it wouldn't slide down. This worked for him. Our minds communicate with us through symbols. It may sound silly, but work with the symbols and images and you'll notice a corresponding difference in your experience.

# Chapter 49
# A Better You

> "People who take charge of their lives…recognize
> that to have experienced circumstances that
> damaged their self-esteem is most unfortunate but to
> allow those circumstances to ruin their lives is tragic
> and unacceptable."
> – *Marilyn Sorensen*

Those who are charismatic don't hold doubts about their competence or efficiency. You can improve your self-image by making a list of what would make you feel more competent or knowledgeable, such as taking classes, joining a health club or an organization associated with your interests, reading about an area you feel deficient in, asking questions of someone you know who has the experience you lack, or practicing a new skill in a less threatening aspect of your life. You may find that you're closer to your desired competency than you thought.

This will also assist you in deciding what you believe and what you stand for, enabling you to get to know and appreciate yourself, increasing your self-esteem and self-respect, broadening your view of life, allowing you to feel more secure in making decisions, and becoming more aware of your talents and available opportunities. You then will not be as reluctant to take further steps, which would also increase your confidence. All of these traits assist in developing your charisma.

You can see yourself more favorably by beginning to change your focus, making a list of your good qualities, strengths, and skills. You may not be aware of the many qualities and skills you do possess. You might utilize the help of a friend or loved one in coming up with these at first. Review them twice a day for thirty days, in sentences beginning with "I am…" or "I can…" Read these statements aloud, with inner conviction, telling yourself that this list represents the truth. Continue adding to this list as you become aware of more strengths or skills. As your focus shifts, you will naturally begin to think of things you can do that you had forgotten about when you weren't focusing in this manner.

To be a better and more charismatic you, clearly define your goals. Then you can understand where you are with these goals and what you need to develop in yourself in order to reach your desires. Those with poor self-images tend to avoid activities they've never done before, because they have not yet attained a level of skill where they will look good to others. You were not born with the ability to use a computer, give a speech, brush your teeth, play tennis, or even walk. Everything you do well, you have practiced. In *Breaking the Chain of Low Self-Esteem* (1998), Marilyn Sorenson offers some logical words of assurance: "While it may be embarrassing to think you are just now learning [a new skill], try to remember that you are the product of your environment – you obviously were never taught this skill or given sufficient opportunity or encouragement to practice." You need to be kind to yourself and give yourself permission to fail, learn, and progress at your own pace. Others will actually admire you for taking such risks.

Brian Tracy (*Action Strategies for Personal Achievement*, 1993) recommends preparing a description of the person you would most like to be in every respect. This description is made up of a combination of all the qualities and attributes that you admire in yourself and in other people. The clearer you are about who you want to become, the more likely you are, day by day, to start moving toward that ideal. Most people tend to have fuzzy or no self-ideals and goals. They give little thought as to what kind of person they wish to be and, therefore, remain stuck in a rut, not making any effort to change or improve. Charismatic people always have goals and ideals that they are moving toward.

Another technique is to change submodalities (Chapter 40). Using the submodalities (specific qualities of your inner images, sounds, and feelings) of whatever it is that you *want* to do well, change the submodalities to those of something you know you can do and do well, something very simple like feed the cat. The submodalities between the two will likely be very different.

To be a better you, a good exercise is to make a list of 101 successes you've experienced in your life. That sounds like a large number of events to come up with. However, it will get you to think more deeply, starting with the obvious successes, and gradually incorporating lesser successes. Accomplishments that you never considered before will arise and you will realize you have achieved more than you thought. When your awareness and focus are on your strengths and successes, your charisma naturally comes out.

✲ ✲ ✲

# Chapter 50
# Presupposed Charisma

> "How many of you have read about Pavlov and his dogs and the bell, and all that stuff?. . . and how many of you are salivating right now?"
> – *Richard Bandler*

In *Using Your Brain for a Change* (1985), Richard Bandler continues, "They had to put the dog in a harness and ring the bell and give it food over and over again to teach it that response. All you did was *read* about it, and you have the same response the dog had." That's how powerful your mind is and how easily and quickly it learns. You can use that power, which is in your imagination, to increase your charisma.

A presupposition is an assumption. It's a belief you adopt that structures your reality and determines your behavior. When you presuppose that you have charisma, you imagine that you have already attained this state, and act as if it were a reality, as if you had already accomplished this goal, feeling what you would feel, hearing what you would hear, seeing what you would see, being charismatic. Presupposing doesn't require any outside knowledge or any analysis or other internal processes, unlike modeling charisma (Chapter 52). It comes completely from pretending that you already know how a state or goal is achieved, without consciously figuring it out.

The significance of presupposing can be illustrated first in relation to trance. There is a theory taught in hypnotherapy classes that professes, "Whatever presupposes trance, causes trance." This was demonstrated by a study where a group of subjects were taken through a formal trance induction and told there was a bowl of fruit on a table in front of them. Then they were asked to take out each piece of fruit one at a time and separate them into piles according to the type of fruit. In a following study, a different group of subjects were asked to merely pretend (without undergoing a formal trance induction) that there was a bowl of fruit on a table in front of them and given the same instructions. These subjects, focusing on the imaginary bowl of fruit and pretending to separate the fruit into stacks, automatically went into a trance state, exhibiting all of the physiological signs of trance. Following these instructions assumed, or presupposed, a trance state (since they had to imagine, or hallucinate – which is a trance phenomenon – a non-existent bowl of fruit) and, therefore, that state actually occurred. Continued focus and suggestion are required to maintain the trance state; however, the trance state was achieved by pretense.

Michael Yapko (*Trancework*, 1990) states that, "A subject may begin by playing at trance behavior, but at a certain, idiosyncratic point along the way, a true trance experience begins." This, explained by Yapko as the "as if" technique, happens when "a person is asked to act 'as if' she can do the thing she feels unable to do (e. g., relax, go into trance) long enough to actually do it and experience what it's like to do it. The issue then becomes one of whether it really matters if the action is real or a pretense if the outcome is the same. . ." He later elaborates that no direct suggestion to the client was involved for her to respond in a particular way, only to act "as if" she were responding in the way suggested. In this example, that would mean suggesting that she respond as if she were relaxed or in a trance, without telling her how to do this.

Demonstrating that the mind cannot tell the difference between something that is real and something that is vividly imagined, the example is often cited to imagine holding a lemon – visualize the lemon in your hand, feel the texture of the lemon, smell the lemon, imagine setting the lemon down and cutting into it with a sharp knife and the juice squirting out. Take a slice of this lemon up to your lips and bite into it. Most people will automatically salivate, even though they know, intellectually, that there is no lemon actually there. The pretense itself bypasses the critical faculty to cause an unconscious, automatic physiological reaction.

If presupposing trance can cause a trance state to occur, then I propose that presupposing charisma can likewise cause a charismatic state, by acting "as if" long enough to experience what it would feel like to be charismatic and responding as if you were charismatic. If you were to act as if you were in a trance, eating a lemon, or were charismatic, the mind and physiology would respond as if it were actually true.

Although you can use the "as if" technique to access unused or undeveloped skills that are blocked in the waking state by unconscious or conscious limitations, some people carry this to the extreme (which I'm not recommending), such as Frank Abignale, Jr., whose life was the basis of the movie *Catch Me If You Can*. Abignale impersonated a teacher, a doctor, and a pilot by pretending he belonged in each profession. It worked; people believed him. However, I'm recommending this process only to access different states of mind.

Dick Clark (*Dick Clark's Program for Success*, 1980) uses this principle for a different purpose. Clark often challenged himself with new projects, for which his previous experience had not given him sufficient preparation. He philosophized that nobody is born with the skill to do his job. However, because of his high profile, if he appeared to be uncertain, those around him would inspect his work with a magnifying glass and watch for any mistake he might make, increasing his stress and undermining his shaky skills. So, he acted confidently, pretending he already had the necessary experience.

Clark explains, "I act as if I really have the situation under control. People then go about their business as usual while I hurry up and learn how the hell to do the job." Clark believes that in almost every skill you first must *do*; then you learn what you're doing. "Since my ego never prevents me from asking stupid questions, I quickly learn to master a situation with an air of composure. Stupid questions asked with confidence appear to be 'deeper than what meets the eye.'" People believed he couldn't possibly be asking such a dumb question, and assumed there must have been a deeper meaning to his query that went beyond their ability to comprehend. They could only answer his questions at face value, convinced they missed the entire thrust of his inquiry. He then calmly accepted the explanation and went about his business, gaining the answers he needed.

# Chapter 51
# Memories – Past and Future

> "The mind does *not* take in experience and store it in exact form for accurate recall later. In fact, memories are stored on the basis of perceptions, and so are subject to the same distortions as perceptions."
> – *Michael Yapko*

Our memories are not as cut and dried as we might think. In *Trancework* (1990), Yapko explains, "People can 'remember' things that did not actually happen, they can remember selected fragments of an experience, and they can take bits and pieces of multiple memories and combine them into one false memory...if you are looking for 'truth,' you are unlikely to find it in memory." In psychotherapy, it is essential to understand how someone represents and accesses past experience. That the memory seems "real" to the person is the main point. It is your *belief* about a memory, and not the memory itself, that creates your feelings and behaviors. The good news is that this means that you can now choose to remember or perceive any event differently at any time you desire.

In *Richard Bandler Doing Richard Bandler* (1987), Richard Bandler asks the seminar attendees if they ever experienced knowing somebody they didn't think liked them and then later found out the person really did like them. Bandler challenges, "We have memories that are wrong all the time. If you're going to have a wrong memory, why not have ones that are useful to you?" Charismatic people tend to have useful memories.

Remember times when you perceive you were or might have been charismatic, even though that might not be the way you originally remembered your experiences. Bandler describes a process of building a behavior or familiar state, while in trance. "Go back to different times of your life and install memories of this behavior every couple of years, so you don't have to do it for the first time – have a history of the experience." Then, before coming out of trance, present post-hypnotic suggestions for accessing this behavior or state in certain future contexts which will be utilized out of trance when desired.

Most people are familiar with using age regression for various reasons in hypnotherapy. Stage hypnotists also use age regression to get people to act like they did when they were children. However, hypnosis can also be used to hypothetically take you into the future – age *pro*gression – and learn about how you did things that you haven't actually done yet, or learn something about yourself that you don't yet know consciously.

Milton Erickson, the grandfather of hypnotherapy, used this technique, calling it "pseudo-orientation in time." He had his patient, in trance, go forward in time and relate to that time as the present. Erickson then asked his patient how she got over her problem – specifically, what he said or did or what she learned or decided that helped her overcome her problem. When the patient gave him the details of the "past" therapy that had helped her, Erickson facilitated amnesia for having done so, and thereby obtained a therapeutic strategy from the patient herself. This technique in itself presupposes that the problem was solved at some point, giving the client's unconscious mind the permission to resolve any internal conflict preventing a resolution, and instructing the unconscious to find an appropriate solution to the problem. This technique can assist you in developing charisma.

This technique also dissociates you from your current situation, allowing you to imagine yourself different from the way you are now, seeing something you might not otherwise see in your current fixed perspective. You enter a trance state when you imagine being your future self, as this bypasses the critical faculty and allows you to believe things you wouldn't believe in your conscious, wakeful state. Additionally, you can use it to "try on" different paths your life may take if you were to make one decision or another, giving you insight as to which decision would give you a more desirable outcome.

A similar technique is taught by Serge King in his Huna classes. King instructs that every major decision you make in your life takes you down a certain path. There is another part of yourself, however, who made a different decision, and that "parallel self" continued life down a different path. For anything that you have ever wanted to do in your life, there is a self who made the decision to do that very thing. Through meditation or trance, connect to the time when you had an opportunity to make a different decision than the one you ultimately made, and follow the life of this other self, which had a different outcome. For our purposes, meditate on another self who made different choices and became charismatic (or more charismatic), and imagine what life is like having taken that different path, experiencing being that charismatic self.

Another approach is to imagine walking into a building that has a long hallway with doors on either side. Each door takes you to a different age in your life. You intuitively pick a door which will take you to a charismatic time in your life. Once you open the door, feel all of the feelings you would have when you are charismatic, and know whatever you need to know to be charismatic now.

The techniques above all presume (or presuppose, if you will) that you are or have been charismatic in the past, present, future, or a parallel life. Many philosophers subscribe to the theory that you become more and more as you consistently see yourself. Therefore, the more you "remember" yourself as being charismatic, the more charismatic you will become.

When discussing charisma, people generally think of others who have charisma. How do you know another person has charisma? It's because of the way you feel when you see or hear this person. If you turn that feeling inward, rather than making it about someone else, you can experience yourself having charisma. This makes it an associated state, when you experience charisma from the inside out, seeing what you would see, hearing what you would hear, and feeling what you would feel when you are charismatic. Remember that feeling. That's a memory that is useful.

# Chapter 52
# Modeling Charisma

> "Let me find someone who's already getting the results that I want and let me find out what that person is doing and do the same things."
> — *Tony Robbins*

In the above quote, Tony Robbins (*Personal Power!* 1993) describes the process of modeling. He uses this technique to speed up the process of attaining results. If you know what you want, instead of just taking random action, you can model the success of someone else who has achieved your goals or similar goals. Robbins continues, "If people succeed, it's because they're doing certain things over and over and over again. And if we do the same kinds of things, we plant the same kinds of seeds, we're gonna reap the same kinds of rewards." What works for one person, should work for anyone.

When you model charisma, you find someone who you feel is already charismatic and discover how the person does it, either by observation or by actually asking the person if he or she is aware of the behavior. Develop a strategy based on the model of this charismatic person to help you to tap into an energy of charisma and a powerful presence. If someone can be charismatic, and you learn how he or she achieves this state, if you were to follow the same steps, then you should be able to be charismatic as well.

You can test this by watching people who are charismatic and duplicating the way they carry themselves, breathe, move, gesture, and use their eyes and facial expressions. You will feel a shift in your thoughts and feelings, and become more charismatic yourself.

Although you can model, or emulate, others, this is done only to understand how charisma is achieved. However, you must figure out how to be yourself while applying what you've learned. You could learn how to be a great singer or a great athlete from studying one you consider to be exceptionally skilled or talented, but at some point – usually after you have internalized your learnings and the skill has been secured at the unconscious level – you must develop your own style and individuality, or you will merely be mimicking. You can be truly charismatic only when it comes from the inside, from who you really are, and when you are claiming your own space and your own personal power.

You can also discover charismatic qualities and model those qualities, rather than an actual person. You can model the physiology, the internal representations, and the self-talk of charisma.

In an e-mail correspondence with my nephew Evan Brainerd, we discussed charismatic qualities concerning his experience with military leaders at the West Point Academy, where he graduated. In relating how these leaders invoke and inspire trust and loyalty with their demeanor, he told me, "A good leader also has a confidence that is innate or developed over considerable experiences with adversity. Their men can sense this confidence, and they will follow it with their lives…wherever they go they bring decisiveness and victory with them. They carry victory and success in the way they talk, walk, and move their body." Similarly, at police academies, an important aspect of training is to develop what they call "command presence." This works together with the uniform to assure the public that they are in control of the situation and to discourage criminal types from crossing their paths. Present moment awareness is also a quality of successful military leaders. As Brainerd says, they "have an uncanny ability to detect the mood of the crowd or the person that they are engaged with. They react to this mood, as they react to their own mood."

# Chapter 52: Modeling Charisma

These qualities, as well as being centered, calm, and composed, can all be meditated upon, modeled, and internalized.

Another approach would be to decide on an outcome, or purpose, and model what you would need to do and who you would need to become in order to accomplish this objective, as outlined below.

1. What do you want to have accomplished when you look back on life in your old age? Some people believe that we are born with a specific purpose to fulfill, and others believe that our purpose is whatever we decide it is. Chapter 37 discussed developing a sense of purpose, which is a good starting point for this process.

2. How would you have to think, speak, and act in order to live that purpose? What habits would you need to cultivate and what would you have to delete from your present life to live out your purpose?

3. What daily choices would you make, attitudes would you have, and activities would you do if you lived as if your purpose meant something to you?

4. How would you live, on a day-to-day basis, if you respected yourself and your life's purpose?

Answering these questions and following the techniques in this chapter will help you to develop the clarity that people with charisma have.

✫ ✫ ✫

# Chapter 53
# Creativity, Playfulness, and Charisma

> "Nobody gives away blue-white diamonds. But you will be frequently offered rocks that can be cut and polished into gems."
> – *Dick Clark*

In the above quote, Dick Clark (*Dick Clark's Program for Success*, 1980) points out that success is rarely just handed to you, but it is often available to you when you "accept that it is your responsibility to clean up the mess that preceded you," and that you need to "be prepared to react to the unconventional challenge" to achieve success. This takes imagination and creativity, which seem to accompany charisma. In my mind, we feel the most charismatic when we are being creative and intuitive, which necessarily means being in the moment. The most charismatic people generally are the most creative, and often use playfulness and humor in communicating. They have removed or diminished blocks in their energy and limits in their thinking, allowing their intuition full range.

Oppenheimer Funds has an advertisement on television where the announcer proclaims that opportunity *doesn't* knock. It sits and waits for the person with the knowledge, skill, and drive to go after it. Charismatic people don't sit back and wait for opportunities; they creatively generate opportunities from their current circumstances or their dreams. This also requires a sense of purpose, decisiveness, and self-motivation.

Creative visualization, done in a state of meditation or self-hypnosis, can open up the imagination. As it bypasses conscious

use meditation and dreams
dream play - active dream — lucid dreams
to generate opportunities

filters, you can just relax and allow whatever images come up to come up. There is no "wrong" way of doing this.

One exercise to assist in sparking your creativity (which can be recorded in advance, so you don't have to memorize it) is to close your eyes, and imagine that there is a forest in front of you. As you walk through the forest, notice the ground, the forest animals, the trees, and the sun shining through the branches, and any sounds or smells that you experience in this setting. You come to a clearing and notice a beach. As you walk down to the beach, see that there is a canoe there, waiting just for you. Get in the canoe and row across the water to a desert island. After tying up the canoe there, walk to a comfortable shady spot where you find a shaman. This shaman is there to answer any questions you have. You can ask the shaman "Abraham" any questions you like about your purpose or any other aspect of your life, and then just listen. Don't try to come up with the right answers or analyze what you hear. Just listen, and know that it will be exactly what you need to hear at this time. When you are done with your conversation, the shaman gives you a gift to take with you. Notice what it is. After thanking your shaman, turn and go back to the canoe, row back to the place you were before, tie up the canoe, go back through the clearing, back through the forest, and to the spot where you started. Finally, come back in the room to now. The answers you received may be from your inner self, your higher self, angels or spirit guides, your higher council, or somewhere else, but that doesn't matter. You will find answers there that you probably never thought of before.

Barbara Sher has a similar, but "waking," process in *It's Only Too Late If You Don't Start Now* (1998), which she calls the "Idea Wizard." In this exercise, you have two chairs. One chair is for you, when you lack ideas to overcome an obstacle or need a creative answer. The other chair is for the Idea Wizard, a special consultant who is paid based on the usable ideas he or she offers you. First, sit in your chair and explain to the other chair, the Idea Wizard, what you want and what your obstacles are. Then get up, change chairs, and become the Idea Wizard. Looking at the first chair, as if you were looking back at you, the questioner, come up with as many creative, workable ideas as you can to meet the goal, motivated by the fact that you get paid only for ideas that are interesting and useful to the questioning you. Then change chairs again and, as you, respond to the ideas from the Wizard, evaluating them as fairly as you can, and explain what you like about the ideas and what you object to in each suggestion. Changing chairs again, use your best ideas to expand on what you liked about the ideas and solve what you objected to. Change back and forth until you're satisfied with the solutions. This dissociates or disconnects your "owning" the problem or situation. When you're the Idea Wizard, you are no longer limited to how you see yourself or what you think you're capable of doing.

Although I didn't include playfulness and humor as components of charisma, I'm presenting them here because they share the expansive energy of charisma. I believe that charisma can be accessed through the magnetic qualities of playfulness and humor for that reason. When you are whimsical, you have a light energy that is not attached to what others think or to being perfect. That makes it easier for you to connect to others.

If you're in an awkward position, which contracts energy, then humor and playfulness will typically help to open that energy up. However, if you're sarcastic, putting somebody down, or using humor inappropriately, that will contract energy.

Many charismatic people are noticeably playful, full of humor, lively, animated, and have a full range of emotional expressiveness. I don't think that playfulness and humor are necessarily exhibited by all charismatic people, but because of the related energy, playfulness and humor complement and enhance charisma. This is probably why many people equate charisma with people who are outgoing and extroverted. There are also powerfully charismatic people who are primarily introverted though. However, they can exhibit a strong sense of humor and playfulness in the communications they offer. These qualities also require imagination and creativity.

People who are joyful are usually quite magnetic. They are people you want to be around, because they lift you up and make you feel better. When you become that joyful person yourself, you make yourself and others feel better, both emotionally and physically. Shelley Stockwell-Nicholas, the president of the International Hypnosis Federation, is the presenter of *Stockwell's Joy Therapy Seminar* and many other workshops ("playshops"), classes, and talks. Her presentations always include laughter, poetry, and songs and are full of light and vibrant energy. You always leave her presence with a smile on your face. She explains in the YouTube. com video interview *Joy Therapy*, "If you can just force a smile, even in the worst of circumstances, you send endorphins to your brain." This will improve your health, make you feel good, and make you irresistible to other people and success.

# Chapter 54
# Success and Charisma

> "Success-oriented people who want to win big see themselves as catalysts, as human agents that can make good things happen."
> – *David J. Schwartz*

Charisma and success often go hand in hand. The magnetism of charisma tends to attract success. Charismatic people tend to be at the top of their chosen professions, and those at the top of their chosen professions tend to be charismatic. Success suggests authority, and authority suggests charisma. This is not always the case; however, more often than not, it is. People who are successful tend to be confident of their abilities, decisive, self-motivated, purposeful, and have a healthy self-esteem, seeing themselves as being successful, responsible, and having empowering beliefs and values. By virtue of their success, they have proven to themselves that they have what it takes to achieve their goals. The most successful people are usually not selfish, but devoted to a purpose that makes the world better for a large segment of the population.

Both successful and charismatic people are typically risk-takers. Taking a risk requires both self-trust and the willingness to make a mistake. You take risks when you stretch out of your comfort zone and do something that has no guarantee attached. In *If Success Is a Game, These Are the Rules* (2000), Cherie Carter-Scott discusses risk-taking. "It means that you do something that is not logical, rational, or reasonable but rather intuitive...Taking a risk is not foolhardy, but it isn't necessarily always sensible, either. It usually lies somewhere in between." Charismatic people trust their own intuition and abilities, as well as the self-motivation to take the necessary actions to make risk-taking pay off.

People who are successful may or may not possess the charismatic qualities of present moment awareness, management of mental and emotional states, or confidence in their private lives. On the other side of the coin, charismatic people may or may not have the knowledge, skill, or business acumen that successful people have.

Success, like any other condition or process you find yourself in, is subjective. Only you can interpret how successful you think you are and what guidelines to use to measure your success. Serge King tells his students to practice seeing everything you do as being successful. You get up in the morning. You did that successfully. You got dressed successfully and successfully arrived at your destination, etc. Even if and when you do something you consider to be unsuccessful, you can turn that around by successfully correcting your error. Before you know it, you will have an awareness of yourself as being successful, and success is charismatic.

A local Huna group I belonged to in the 1980s started each weekly meeting in a circle. Going around the room, everyone said something positive that happened to them that week. There would be a snowball effect, as many people would tell stories that would trigger the minds of others who had experienced similar events, but didn't consider them significant until someone else had brought them up. If you are used to considering what is wrong in your life or in the world as a whole, this is an approach that can help you change your focus to what is right, and create more positive events from this positive focus.

By now, you can understand how someone could have it all and still be unhappy. No matter how good your life is, you can always focus on something that isn't perfect or doesn't match your expectations. Failure is being able to find pain no matter how good everything is in your life. The bottom line is that you have the power right now to make decisions about what to focus on and what interpretations you make.

In *Confidence: Finding It and Living It* (1995), Barbara DeAngelis relates a story about a man with a self-defeating attitude. This man loved running and set a goal for himself to run a four-minute mile. Every morning he'd run, look at his watch, and feel like a failure that he didn't reach that goal. "And instead of feeling confident because he commits to running every day and stays in good shape, he beats himself up." DeAngelis insists you should honor the efforts you make in self-improvement or goals, and not put off feeling good about yourself until you've reached perfection. Instead of thinking, "I'll feel really good about myself when…" replace that thought with, "Right now, I feel really good about myself, because…" Doing so will give you a success consciousness that is prevalent in those with charisma.

Sometimes people are successful in the eyes of others, but not in their own eyes. If you don't feel successful or see yourself as successful, it doesn't matter what other people think. It also doesn't matter what other people think, as long as you see everything you do as being successful and experience the energy of being successful and charismatic. It's all about you and the way you interpret your own life.

✵ ✵ ✵

# Chapter 55
# Starting Now

> "With greater confidence in yourself and your
> abilities, you will set bigger goals, make bigger plans,
> and commit yourself to achieving objectives that
> today you only dream about."
> – *Brian Tracy*

You can increase your charisma and your success starting right now. This chapter highlights some of the main concepts in this book.

Charisma is a state and an outward expression of a self-empowering belief system. You project how you feel about yourself and the world by your confidence, self-esteem, sense of purpose, decisiveness, and self-motivation.

You communicate personal power unconsciously by the way you see yourself and the way you interpret people and events around you. You have a certain internal representational system in which you tell yourself certain things and have certain internal images, sounds, feelings, and self-talk. Your body language and verbal language corresponds with your belief system and internal representations.

As charisma is a state, there are subtle degrees of charisma (just like when you are in a happy state you can be a little happy, very happy, ecstatic, and any degree in between). Additionally, your belief system (which is based on your past experiences and programming) affects your values. People who have different beliefs and values will see the same person differently, and may come to different conclusions about that person. Charisma is subjective, both by the person who is being evaluated and the person or people doing the evaluating. Generally, however, the more congruent you are in your belief system and values and the more solidly you meet the criteria set forth in this book, the more you will be considered to be charismatic.

You do not always maintain the same state or the same degree of that particular state, although typically, you have habitual states in given situations. Your belief system is also different for different situations and circumstances, and you see yourself differently in the different roles you play in your life, which become habitual as well. Similarly, your level of confidence, self-esteem, decisiveness, and self-motivation vary depending on where you are and what you are doing. You may be confident in an acting role that is scripted, but not in a one-on-one social conversation that is not scripted. Conversely, you may have beliefs about yourself that make you fear speaking in public, preventing you from being a charismatic presenter, yet feel quite comfortable and be charismatic conversing in a social situation.

People who are charismatic give an impression of aliveness, which you can have only when you are fully focused in the present moment. One of the traits of charismatic people is that they are tuned into their environment and aware of people, places, and events around them. Because they are so present, they can appear to be psychic, since they are aware of details in the behavior of people around them and they see current situations more clearly than most people. They are not distracted by rehashing the past or planning the future (as most people are most of the time), with the exception of times that they set aside specifically for that purpose. They are also highly intuitive because of their awareness of their own internal feelings, their own behavior, and the behavior of others.

You can tell whether or not a person is present with you by looking into his or her eyes. The eyes of a charismatic person always sparkle with an alertness and involvement. Most people have their energy fragmented, with their minds drifting between several different places in space and time. The more energy you have focused where you are right now, the more energy you will have access to, which gives you a powerful appearance of intense magnetism. Therefore, it would make sense that you would have the highest level of personal power when you are fully in the present moment.

When you are charismatic, you appear to be on a mission. The great majority of charismatic people have a distinct sense of purpose.

Charismatic people take the position that even though events and people are out of their control, there are always conditions that are under their control. If you didn't believe that you had some power to effect change, there would be no reason to have a sense of purpose. If nothing else, you always have control over your interpretation of a situation and how you choose to respond.

People who are charismatic tend to be powerfully calm, focused, and centered (mentally and emotionally balanced). These attributes all correlate to states. Events outside of your control are constantly occurring, and so in order to be charismatic, you must be able to utilize whatever happens in a way that you are operating from a position of your strengths. People who attempt to control situations and other people usually do so because they do not feel any personal power or inner control. Charismatic people do not typically attempt to control, but they utilize whatever comes their way. For the most part, they realize that the only control they have is internal, and they work from that perspective.

Focus is important to any achievement, as your reality is based on your focus. If you focus on your lacks or what you don't want, this is the direction you will move in. If you focus on your strengths and what you do want in your life or your best personality traits and behaviors, this is what will be intensified and increased. There will always be both positive and negative at any given time. You can choose what you focus on and what you multiply in your life.

Perfection does not exist. If you are focused only on dealing with obstacles or perceived obstacles, you will never realize success, as you will always find another problem to replace any problem you solve. However, when you focus on the outcome or reward, you will soon see continual progress, if not outright success. Since charismatic people are focused on their sense of purpose, they are constantly moving forward.

You tend to focus on what you identify with. Obviously, if you are only focused on your faults, you will believe that is who you are and you will notice every time you exhibit those faults. You then fail to notice whenever you do something productive and the many opportunities that are constantly presenting themselves to you that will help develop your skills and charismatic qualities.

However, when you focus on the charismatic qualities you want to develop, presuppose that you already have these qualities, or model the strategies of someone with these qualities, you will begin to identify more with the qualities you desire and see places where you have already displayed these characteristics. You will also see where and how you can apply them to a greater extent.

To paraphrase Abraham Maslow, you will change only when your awareness of yourself changes.

✳ ✳ ✳

# Appendix: Beginning Chapter Quotes

1) "The speech was nothing, but the man's presence was everything. It was electrical, magnetic." – A New York politician's observation of Theodore Roosevelt (as quoted by Ronald E. Riggio, *The Charisma Quotient*, 1987)

2) "What is necessary to change a person is to change his awareness of himself." – Abraham Maslow (as quoted by Wayne Dyer, *Inspiration: Your Ultimate Calling*, 2006)

3) "My patients are my patients because they are out of rapport with their unconscious minds." – Milton Erickson (hypnotherapy class)

4) "A magnetic personality is *not* something we can see – but something we *feel.*" – Ben Sweetland (*I Can,* 1953)

5) "A tentative person will walk tentatively, almost questioning the ground at every step. A jaunty walker often turns out to be happy-go-lucky, and so on." – Julius Fast (*The Body Language of Sex, Power & Aggression,* 1977)

6) "The fastest way to change your identity is to change the way you move – your face, your body, your voice. Because [that sends] a signal to your brain that you're behaving differently, and it starts to get you to think differently." – Tony Robbins (*The Power to Shape Your Destiny,* 2001)

7) "A happy person is not a person in a certain set of circumstances, but rather a person with a certain set of attitudes." – Hugh Downs (as quoted by Lauren Luria, *Take Charge of Your Life Today,* 2001)

8) "There are two primary choices in life: to accept conditions as they exist, or accept the responsibility for changing them." – Denis Waitley (*The Psychology of Winning,* 1987)

9) "The sum total of all of your choices, both conscious and unconscious, has led you to where you are today." – Tad James

(*The Accelerated Neuro-Linguistic Programming Practitioner Training Pre-Study Program*, 2006)

10) "The more files we have in our mental filing cabinet, which tell us something about ourselves, the more we will attract and accept other thoughts and ideas which support and prove what is already stored in our files." – Shad Helmstetter (*What to Say When You Talk to Yourself*, 1982)

11) "If values are not aligned with the changes you made… then typically the changes will regress." – Tad James and Wyatt Woodsmall (*Time Line Therapy and the Basis of Personality*, 1988)

12) "It's important to understand that any limit to your thinking exists only in the paradigms ingrained in you, not in your potential or your ability to create a big vision." – Loral Langemeier (*The Millionaire Maker*, 2006)

13) "Successes are boring, because they only confirm what you already know. Failures are much more interesting, because they indicate where you can learn something new." – Richard Bandler (Foreword of *Change Your Mind and Keep the Change* by Steve Andreas and Connirae Andreas, 1987)

14) "Understanding the energy consequences of our thoughts and beliefs, as well as our actions, may force us to become honest to a new degree." – Caroline Myss (*Anatomy of the Spirit*, 1996)

15) "If you've identified now limiting decisions that you've got in your life, get excited! Because that means that we're on our way to a breakthrough." – Christopher Howard (*Your Personal Breakthrough*, 2006)

16) "Every practitioner of hypnosis will certify that success depends on your feeling of certainty, of 'I can.'" – Kurt Tepperwien (*Master Secrets of Hypnosis and Self-Hypnosis*, 1991)

17) "We are already in trance – clients come to us because they're stuck in a trance that no longer serves their lives. So, our job is not to induce trance, but to shift it." – Dan Cleary ("Induction

and Intent," lecture at the American Board of Hypnotherapy Convention, Newport Beach, CA, February 2002)

18) "We hear what we listen for." – Kermit L. Long (as quoted by Richard Bolles, *The Three Boxes of Life*, 1981)

19) "For all our insight, obstinate habits do not disappear until replaced by other habits...No amount of confession and no amount of explaining can make the crooked plant grow straight; it must be trained upon the trellis by the gardener's art." – Carl Jung (as quoted by Wayne Dyer, *Inspiration: Your Ultimate Calling*, 2006)

20) "The person with low self-esteem discards the positive while actually 'enlarging' and 'enhancing' those tape sequences containing unfavorable personal information." – Marilyn Sorensen (*Breaking the Chain of Low Self-Esteem*, 1998)

21) "What if, instead of considering this 'wasted' time, you shifted your response and considered the wait 'found' time – a surprise gift, like finding a ten-dollar bill in the pocket of a coat you haven't worn since last year?" – Stephan Rechtschaffen (*Time Shifting*, 1996)

22) "What we say to ourselves dictates how we feel, what we believe, and ultimately what we do...It is actually here in our minds that we form our interpretations and give ourselves feedback, through our inner voice." – Marilyn Sorensen (*Breaking the Chain of Low Self-Esteem*, 1998)

23) "The quality of your life comes down to the quality of the questions you ask yourself on a daily basis." – Tony Robbins (*Personal Power!* 1993)

24) "Every atom is more than 99. 9999 percent empty space, and the subatomic particles moving at lightning speed through this space are actually bundles of vibrating energy. These vibrations aren't random and meaningless, however; they carry information." – Deepak Chopra (*Quantum Healing*, 1989)

25) "Grok means chewing on a concept and assimilating it until it becomes one with you and your understanding rather

than swallowing it whole and half-digested." – Lama Surya Das (*Awakening the Buddha Within*, 1997)

26) "Charisma is a matter of expanding your sense of self to embrace all the people with whom you come in contact." – Roger Dawson (*13 Secrets of Power Performance*, 1994)

27) "The past does not equal the future, unless you live there." – Tony Robbins (*The Power to Shape your Destiny*, 2001)

28) "In my seminars, I know I've captured the right rhythm when I am actually so present that I'm not consciously monitoring what I'm saying – I am just 'being' in the flow of speaking." – Stephan Rechtschaffen (*Time Shifting*, 1996)

29) "You are not stuck in life; you are stuck in what you've told yourself life is about." – Guy Finley (*Secrets of Being Unstoppable*, 2005)

30) "Our spirits, our energy, and our personal power are all one and the same force." – Caroline Myss (*Anatomy of the Spirit*, 1996)

31) "When someone...feels driven to do something he doesn't consciously want to do, we assume that an 'unconscious part' makes him do it." – Connirae and Steve Andreas (*Heart of the Mind*, 1989)

32) "Tibetan Buddhism says that at the heart of you, me, every single person...is an inner radiance that reflects our essential nature. . ." – Lama Surya Das (*Awakening the Buddha Within*, 1997)

33) "Every brain state, every emotional state, has a corresponding brainwave pattern and breath pattern...If you adopt the breathing pattern of a relaxed person, you literally fool the body...into thinking it's relaxed." – Marc David (*Mind/Body Nutrition*, 2006)

34) "Regular meditation assists you in reconnecting to the aspect of your inner self that is connected to God." – John Gray (*How to Get What You Want and Want What You Have*, 1999)

35) "When I used to coach singing clients on how to overcome self-doubt or stage fright, I would simply have them switch

their focus away from their personal feelings about themselves and how they are doing, and onto...the interpretation of the song." – Nijole Sparkis (e-mail interview with author, 2008)

36) "Fritz Perls, the father of Gestalt psychology, coined the somewhat paradoxical phrase 'trying fails, awareness cures' to make the point that the harder we try, the more confused things often become, and that the remedy for 'trying too hard' is to be found in simple awareness." – Barry Green (*The Inner Game of Music*, 1986)

37) "You're here. Therefore, there's a purpose." – Serge King (*The Most Important Thing*, 1988)

38) "To master ourselves is to arrive home at the center of being. . . What we seek, we already *are*." – Lama Surya Das (*Awakening the Buddha Within*, 1997)

39) "All the emotions that you could ever have are nothing but physiological storms in your brain. Put your body in the right place, focus on things the right way, you feel them now." – Tony Robbins (*Live With Passion!*, 1998)

40) "The swish pattern has a more powerful effect than any other technique I've used...It's a very generative pattern that programs your brain to go in a new direction." – Richard Bandler (*Using Your Brain for a Change*, 1985)

41) "When you become aware of the amount of energy within you, you can focus it in a particular direction, with specific intention, and you give it specific qualities." – Tad James and David Shepherd (*Presenting Magically*, 2001)

42) "There are definitely times when I feel less charisma or "magic" on stage than other times...I usually blame it on quality of sleep, food, or just plain old mood. But charisma is different than just a good show." – Kyle Vincent (interview, October 28, 2008)

43) "True confidence...comes from a commitment you make to yourself, a commitment that you will do whatever it is that you want and need to do in life." – Barbara DeAngelis (*Confidence: Finding It and Living It*, 1995)

44) "Each decision we make, whether large or small, defines who we are and the quality of person we are becoming." – Valerie Wells (*Naturally Powerful*, 1999)

45) "You choose only what you believe is possible to choose, and these choices determine what you do with your life and who you become." – Grandmaster Tai Yun Kim (*Seven Steps to Inner Power*, 1991)

46) "The people who step up to the plate and actually swing the bat are the ones who are in the game and ultimately the ones who score. If you don't swing at the ball, how can you ever expect to hit a home run?" – Cherie Carter-Scott (*If Success Is a Game, These Are the Rules*, 2000)

47) "...by being strong, [you] must be willing to take the consequences of that power and let go of the pretense, however unconsciously buried, that [you] are helpless. Perhaps it is easier to believe we have little potential than to admit our talents." – Marsha Sinetar (*Do What You Love, The Money Will Follow*, 1987)

48) "One's self-esteem is the subjective assessment of one's value as a human being. It is formed in part by the feedback one gets from others, but it is formed to a large extent by one's belief system." – Michael Yapko (*Trancework*, 1990)

49) "...people who take charge of their lives...recognize that to have experienced circumstances that damaged their self-esteem is most unfortunate but to allow those circumstances to ruin their lives is tragic and unacceptable." – Marilyn Sorensen (*Breaking the Chain of Low Self-Esteem*, 1998)

50) "How many of you have read about Pavlov and his dogs and the bell, and all that stuff?. . . and how many of you are salivating right now?" – Richard Bandler (*Using Your Brain For a Change*, 1985)

51) "The mind does *not* take in experience and store it in exact form for accurate recall later. In fact, memories are stored on the basis of perceptions, and so are subject to the same distortions as perceptions." – Michael Yapko (*Trancework*, 1990)

52) "Let me find someone who's already getting the results that I want and let me find out what that person is doing and do the same things." – Tony Robbins (*Personal Power!* 1993)

53) "Nobody gives away blue-white diamonds. But you will be frequently offered rocks that can be cut and polished into gems." – Dick Clark (*Dick Clark's Program for Success,* 1980)

54) "Success-oriented people who want to win big see themselves as catalysts, as human agents that can make good things happen." – David J. Schwartz (*The Magic of Getting What You Want,* 1983)

55) "With greater confidence in yourself and your abilities, you will set bigger goals, make bigger plans, and commit yourself to achieving objectives that today you only dream about." – Brian Tracy (Nightingale-Conant e-mail "Motivational Quote of the Day," December 23, 2008)

# Bibliography

Allen, David, *Getting Things Done Fast: The Ultimate Stress-Free Productivity System*, Niles, Illinois, Nightingale-Conant audio tape seminar, 2001

Andreas, Connirae and Steve, *Heart of the Mind*, Moab, Utah, Real People Press, 1989

Andreas, Connirae and Steve, *Change Your Mind and Keep the Change*, Moab, Utah, Real People Press, 1987

Bandler, Richard, *Personal Outcomes: Changing Responses*, Evergreen, Colorado, NLP Comprehensive, DVD seminar, 1989

Bandler, Richard *Personal Outcomes: Motivation*, Evergreen, Colorado, NLP Comprehensive, DVD seminar, 1989

Bandler, Richard, *Personal Outcomes: Resolving Problems*, Evergreen, Colorado, NLP Comprehensive, DVD seminar, 1989

Bandler, Richard, Ed Reese and Ed Uzee co-presenters, *Rare Bandler*, Indiana Rocks Beach, Florida, Southern Institute Press, Inc., video tape seminar, 1982.

Bandler, Richard, and Ed Reese, co-presenters, *Richard Bandler Doing Richard Bandler*, videotape seminar, Southern Institute Press, Inc., Indiana Rocks Beach, Florida, 1987

Bandler, Richard, *Using Your Brain for a Change*, Maob, Utah, Real People Press, 1985

Bolles, Richard N., *The Three Boxes of Life*, Berkeley, Ten Speed Press, 1981

Brenckman, Richard, "Change Your Channel", *Avatar Journal* (Volume XII, Issue 1), Altamonte Springs, Star's Edge International, 1998

Carter-Scott, Cherie, *If Success Is a Game, These Are the Rules*, New York, Broadway Books, 2000

Chopra, Deepak, M. D., *Quantum Healing*, New York, Bantam Books, 1989

Chopra, Deepak, M. D., *Ageless Body, Timeless Mind*, New York, Harmony Books, 1993

Clark, Dick, *Dick Clark's Program for Success*, New York, Cornerstone Library, 1980

Cleary, Daniel, "Induction and Intent", lecture at the American Board of Hypnotherapy Convention, Newport Beach, California, February 2002

Cousins,_Norman, *Anatomy of an Illness*, New York, W. W. Norton & Co., Inc., 1979

Das, Lama Surya, *Awakening the Buddha Within*, New York, Broadway Books, 1997

DeAngelis, Barbara, *Confidence: Finding It and Living It*, Carson, California, Hay House, 1995

Dyer, Wayne W., PhD, *Inspiration: Your Ultimate Calling*, Carlsbad, CA, Hay House, Inc., 2006

Elman, Dave, *Hypnotherapy*, Glendale, Westwood Publishing, 1964

Fiore, Neil, *Conquering Procrastination*, Niles, Illinois, Nightingale-Conant audio tape series, 1995

Frankl, Viktor, *Man's Search for Meaning*, Boston, Beacon Press, 1963

Gindes, Bernard C., M. D., *New Concepts of Hypnosis*, North Hollywood, Wilshire Book Company, 1951

Gray, John, *How to Get What You Want and Want What You Have*, New York, Harper Collins Publishers, 1999

Green, Barry with W. Timothy Gallwey, *The Inner Game of Music*, New York, Doubleday, 1986

Hall, Nick, PhD, *Change Your Beliefs, Change Your Life*, Niles, Illinois, Nightingale-Conant Audio tape series, 2000

Hall, Nick, Y*our Beliefs and Your Health – Your Personal Guide*, Niles, Illinois, Nightingale-Conant, 2000

Hanh, Thich Nhat, *The Present Moment*, Boulder, Sounds True Recordings, audio tape series, 1994

Helmstetter, Shad, *What to Say When You Talk to Your Self*, New York, Pocket Books, 1982

Huxley, Parthenon, "Bazooka Joe", Big Groovy Music, BMI/MCA Music Publishing, 1994

James, Tad, *Deep Trance Phenomena*, Honolulu, Advanced Neuro Dynamics, Inc., audio tape series, 1996

James, Tad and David Shephard, *Presenting Magically*, Bethel, CT, Crown House Publishing Company LLC, 2001

James, Tad and Wyatt Woodsmall, *Time Line Therapy and the Basis of Personality*, Cupertino, Meta Publications, 1988

Kabat-Zinn, Jon, *Wherever You Go, There You Are*, New York, Hyperion, 1994

Kim, Grandmaster Tai Yun, *Seven Steps to Inner Power*, San Rafael, CA, New World Library, 1991

King, Serge, *Mastering Your Hidden Self*, Wheaton, IL, A Quest Book, 1985

King, Serge, *Positive Programming*, Princeville, Hawaii, Hunacom, audio tape lecture, 1988

King, Serge, *The Most Important Thing*, Princeville, Hawaii, Hunacom, audio tape lecture, 1988

King, Serge, *The Seven Principles of Huna*, Kilauea, Hunacom, video, 1987

Luria, Lauren, *Take Charge of Your Life Today*, Palm Springs, Personal Coach Network, 2001

Maisel, Eric, *Fearless Creating*, New York, G. P. Putnam's Sons, 1995

McLaughlin, Peter, *Unlimited Energy*, Morton Grove, Illinois, Nightingale-Conant, audio tape series, 1998

Michaelson, Geoff, *ABD Survival Guide* (e-mail newsletter), "The Power of One Word," August 15, 2001

Myss, Caroline, *Anatomy of the Spirit*, New York, Three Rivers Press, 1996

Rechtschaffen, Stephan, *Time Shifting*, New York, Doubleday, 1996

Robbins, Anthony, *Personal Power!* San Diego, Robbins Research International, Inc., 1993

Robbins, Anthony, *The Power to Shape Your Destiny*, Niles, Illinois, Nightingale Conant, audio tape series, 2001

Robbins, Anthony, *Unleash the Power Within*, Niles, Illinois, Nightingale Conant, audio tape series, 1999

Sher, Barbara, *How to Live the Life you Love*, Boulder, Sounds True Catalog, audio workshop, 1996

Sher, Barbara, *It's Only Too Late If You Don't Start Now*, New York, Delacorte Press, 1998

Sinetar, Marsha, *Do What You Love, The Money Will Follow*, New York City, Dell Publishing, 1987

Sorensen, Marilyn J., *Breaking the Chain of Low Self-Esteem*, Sherwood, Oregon, Wolf Publishing Co., 1998

Steinfeld, Jake, *Power Living by Jake*, New York, Random House, 1997

Sweetland, Ben, *I Can*, New York, Cadillac Publishing Company Inc., 1953

Tolle, Eckhart, *Realizing the Power of Now*, Boulder, Sounds True Catalog, audio workshop, 2003

Tracy, Brian, *Action Strategies for Personal Achievement*, Niles, Illinois, Nightingale Conant audio tape series, 1993

Wells, Valerie, *Naturally Powerful*, New York, A Perigee Book, 1999

Yapko, Michael D., *Trancework*, New York, Brunner/Mazel Publishers, 1990

# Index

# About the Author

Dr. Gia (pronounced GEE-uh) Brainerd has been studying mind technologies, including psychology, meditation, Huna, hypnosis, NLP (Neuro-Linguistic Programming), and energy medicine for thirty-five years. She has been fascinated with theater and music since she was a child and developed numerous friendships with people associated with the performing arts. In the 1980s, Gia followed the Los Angeles/Hollywood music scene, publishing and writing for *Behind the Music* (a magazine predating, and not associated with, the popular television series). She interviewed people in the industry and gained insight into why some entertainers connected with their audiences and others did not.

In the 1990s, Gia began her post-graduate studies at the American Institute of Hypnotherapy, later transferring to American Pacific University, where she earned her PhD in clinical hypnotherapy. Her clientele primarily consists of entertainers.

Gia is a member of The American Board of Hypnotherapy and The International Hypnosis Federation.

3048213

Made in the USA